THE
PUBLIC
DOMAIN
CODE BOOK

www.publicdomaincodebook.com

TONY LAIDIG

(EXPLORER AND TREASURE HUNTER)

NEW YORK

The Public Domain Code Book
by Tony Laidig
www.publicdomaincodebook.com
tony@thepublicdomainexpert.com

ISBN: 1-60037-138-8 (Paperback)
ISBN: 1-60037-139-6 (eBook)

Published by:

MORGAN · JAMES
THE ENTREPRENEURIAL PUBLISHER ™

Habitat
for Humanity®
Peninsula
Building Partner

Morgan James Publishing, LLC
1225 Franklin Ave Ste 325
Garden City, NY 11530-1693
Toll Free 800-485-4943
www.MorganJamesPublishing.com

Cover and Interior Design by:
Tony Laidig
www.thecoverexpert.com
tony@thecoverexpert.com

The Old Fisherman's Net **edited by:**
Jeanette Sprecher
Sprecher Writing Services

LEGAL NOTICE

All images, logos, products, names and websites reproduced herein are copyright of their respective businesses.

This book is presented for information and research purposes only and was designed to provide accurate and authoritative information with regard to the subject matter covered. It is sold with the understanding that the publisher and author are not engaged in rendering legal, accounting, or other professional advice. The material contained within also does not in any way constitute professional advice and should not be perceived as such.

If legal advice or other professional assistance is required, the services of a competent professional should be sought. The reader is also advised to consult with an appropriately qualified professional before making any business decisions related to the information contained herein.

The author, Tony Laidig, does not accept any responsibility for any liabilities resulting from business decisions made by purchasers of this book. We make no claim that you will earn any income using this book whatsoever. Income results can vary based upon the reader's personal business practices, hard work and other benefits or strategies. You must assume the risk that you will not earn any income from this product or its use.

"All the glory of the world would be buried in oblivion, unless God had provided mortals with the remedy of books."

—Bishop Richard De Bury

THE PUBLIC DOMAIN CODE BOOK
DECODED WORDSEARCH

```
A G P E S M O C S G A R K O O B G S M U O K
Q S U X U P C C E L O R G C A M W O W F G E
C O H T Y R L Y A N C Q M A O P C T H K N S
C I D V E F I V M R Z Y O C N T L I A Q I S
W L Z B H N Y S T C A B D A N R D V L I G I
T A F H U E B A K S M N X I A I R T O K R N
E N Y A M N D E Z O I V R B P F B E C V O G
L D O W A X I C R F D P D M D B O R G M O E
D H L M N R A X O G D A M O D I R P O O T R
R E A H I K C I N A O U T Y I B M C V N O P
I A E P S X L H E A Z R R A S L X O P M H U
T L D S T B W R I X S X G A C I V G L O P B
C T I X I T G Z V V S A S U R O E M W C D L
H H T B C C J P N O E X G T D M M C O A P I
P O E O T M E T T N K O I O N A O B L M Z S
R R C R E R P A I D L L R T V N P Q W A F H
E G N G X F U K S H A S P G P I L Z F R J I
S N E W T H O U G H T L I B R A R Y C O M N
S A T M S N L S O R T N O M L C T Y X H A G
O M D G O Z N B V U E D B I L O I B P T S C
R K N J R D X D W M A R W B E M E Y V U O O
G L V O G S P N A P L I T F I X C O M A L M
```

Contained within this wordsearch are 24 Public Domain website addresses. The websites represent a variety of different types of Public Domain resources that are available. And, as an added twist to the wordsearch, a few of the websites hidden in the wordsearch are only revealed in the puzzle. You will not find them listed anywhere else in this book. Some of the websites will be obvious, some not so obvious. So have fun...and good luck!

    - 5 -   *www.publicdomaincodebook.com*

CONTENTS

❧❦

Copyright Term Quick Reference Guide

Definition: A public domain work is a creative work that is not protected by copyright and which may be freely used by everyone. The reasons that the work is not protected include:
(1) the term of copyright for the work has expired;
(2) the author failed to satisfy statutory formalities to perfect the copyright or
(3) the work is a work of the U.S. Government.

DATE OF WORK:	PROTECTION BEGINS:	TERM:
Published before 1923	**In public domain**	None
Published from 1923 - 63	When published with notice[3]	28 years + could be renewed for 47 years, now extended by 20 years for a total renewal of 67 years. **If not so renewed, now in public domain**
Published from 1964 - 77	When published with notice	28 years for first term; now automatic extension of 67 years for second term
Created before 1-1-78 but not published	1-1-78, the effective date of the 1976 Act which eliminated common law copyright	Life + 70 years or 12-31-2002, whichever is greater
Created before 1-1-78 but published between then and 12-31-2002	1-1-78, the effective date of the 1976 Act which eliminated common law copyright	Life + 70 years or 12-31-2047, whichever is greater
Created 1-1-78 or after	When work is fixed in tangible medium of expression	Life + 70 years[1] (or if work of corporate authorship, the shorter of 95 years from publication, or 120 years from creation[2])

1. Term of joint works is measured by life of the longest-lived author.
2. Works for hire, anonymous and pseudonymous works also have this term. 17 U.S.C. § 302(c).
3. Under the 1909 Act, works published without notice went into the public domain upon publication. Works published without notice between 1-1-78 and 3-1-89, effective date of the Berne Convention Implementation Act, retained copyright only if efforts to correct the accidental omission of notice was made within five years, such as by placing notice on unsold copies. 17 U.S.C. § 405. (Notes courtesy of Professor Tom Field, Franklin Pierce Law Center and Lolly Gasaway)

INTRODUCTION

✤

I have always been fascinated with treasure and treasure hunting. I do not know if it was about the money, the thrill of the hunt or the excitement of trying to solve a mystery. I remember spending hours trying to solve the 1885 Beale Ciphers—one of which allegedly states the location of a buried treasure of gold and silver estimated to be worth over 20 million US dollars in today's money.

I also think back on my trip to New York City, convinced I had **solved the puzzle** in the 1984 release, "Treasure: In Search of the Golden Horse," where I had hoped to discover the 1 kilogram golden horse that was buried in a box somewhere on public land within the continental United States. Of course, I didn't solve the Beale Ciphers and I didn't find the golden horse (although I spent a lovely day digging around under the Queensboro Bridge). But those disappointments never quenched the fire that burned within me to discover. I know that passion for hidden treasure will always be a part of who I am. I AM a seeker of secrets…a solver of mysteries and a revealer of the hidden, and I believe those passions have become the foundation for my love of the Public Domain.

The Public Domain, in my opinion, represents the ultimate treasure hunt. It literally contains more treasures than you or I could ever discover and enjoy in several lifetimes. Perhaps you are wondering, "Well **what** exactly IS the Public Domain, and **where** do I find this treasure?" I'll explain what the Public Domain is in just a moment, but first, I want to let you know that the "where" is in your hands…**right now**.

My introduction to the Public Domain began 20 years ago when I started reproducing old maps to sell. I managed a commercial printing company at the time and had access to all the printing equipment I needed to create quality reproductions. The maps sold well, and that experience led me to reproduce other "old" items like photographs and artwork. The demand was amazing. We didn't have the benefit of the Internet in those days and our "Ebay" was an outdoor flea market in Smithsville, New Jersey. But during those times, our "Public Domain" sales really helped pay the bills. We made thousands of dollars!

 www.publicdomaincodebook.com

It wasn't until the past few years that I reconnected with Public Domain content. I believe it was an article by Joe Vitale that rekindled the flame in me...and so the search began once again. I noticed how different Internet marketers would talk about the Public Domain and what you could do with it, but they never REALLY told you where to find it. Sure, they provided a few websites to search, but it seemed to me that the really GOOD ones were being kept secret. I began to spend hours pouring through search engine results and following rabbit trails. I wanted to find the sites that the gurus were not talking about. It became an obsession. I spent hundreds, perhaps even, thousands of hours of research and made amazing discoveries. I came across websites where I would think, *I wonder why the gurus don't talk about this website...it's awesome.* Then it hit me..."they" have to know about this one...this must be another one of the gem sites.

So after spending months on my quest for the secret sites, I have compiled my discoveries into this book you are now reading. I have found websites that NO ONE else is talking about...sites that have NEVER been mentioned in any other Public Domain resource (I own nearly all of them). And, with a count of over 200 websites, *The Public Domain Code Book* is also one of the largest collections of Public Domain links anywhere—online or offline.

WHAT THIS BOOK IS AND IS NOT

The Public Domain Code Book is a true "code book" that helps you decipher the clues and directions hidden around the Internet so that you can truly experience the great gold rush of the 21st century. It is also a treasure map...the ultimate treasure map that leads to a vast store of Public Domain gems. The gems are out there awaiting your discovery on websites all over the Internet and around the world. This book will not only connect you with actual Public Domain resources, but will also lead you down a number of "roads less traveled" where you will learn more covert ways to locate Public Domain resources from both online and offline sources as well.

This book is NOT meant to be a "how to" book per se, even though we have provided instructions on how to use each section. It will not provide you with step-by-step instructions on how to develop and polish your gems into cash-producing resources. There are other wonderful resources available to teach you that as well. THIS BOOK'S PURPOSE is to tell you WHERE to find the treasure—and that information is worth millions...literally. I could have easily named the book, "Public Domain Millions," without exaggerating one bit.

WHAT IS PUBLIC DOMAIN?

So now that you're excited and know **where** to begin, let's talk about what you will be looking for. Let's look at just what "Public Domain" is. Wikipedia defines "Public Domain" as follows:

"The public domain comprises the body of knowledge and innovation (especially creative works such as writing, art, music, and inventions) in relation to which no person or other legal entity can establish or maintain proprietary interests. This body of information and creativity is considered to be part of the common cultural and intellectual heritage of humanity, which in general **anyone may use or exploit**. If an item is not in the public domain, this may be the result of a proprietary interest as represented by a copyright or patent. The extent to which members of the public may use or exploit an item in relation to which proprietary interests exist is generally limited. However, when copyright or patent restrictions expire, works will enter the public domain and **may be used by anyone for any purpose**." *(emphasis added)*

(Wikipedia Website; http://en.wikipedia.org/wiki/Public_domain; Accessed 3/7/06)

What that means for you and me is that when the copyright or patent expires on a creative work (book, work of art, etc.), anyone may freely use that work LEGALLY in any manner they choose without the obligation of paying royalties to the creator of the work. This is HUGE...it's like legalized stealing except that it IS legal, so no trips to confession are required.

Now...as you would imagine, there are some parameters you have to work within...some laws that define just what is and what is not considered Public Domain. But don't let that scare you. We have included a quick reference guide to help you determine **easily** whether or not your discoveries are indeed in the Public Domain. We have also included some excellent information sites at the end of the book where you can learn more about the ins and outs of the Public Domain.

PUBLIC DOMAIN ALCHEMY

There are many wonderful ways you can use Public Domain content to make money. This book's primary focus is about discovery not product creation. HOWEVER, here is a quick list of over 15 ways to turn your **book** discoveries into pure gold. (This doesn't even include what you can do with artwork, photographs, maps, etc.)

- Republish as-is in print form

- Republish as-is as a downloadable e-book

- Republish as-is along with other books on CD

- Use content to develop Study Course with workbook

- Use content to develop How-to Course

- Videotape How-to Courses or Training Classes

- Update or rewrite material for new product

- Use portions of different books to create new thematic "collection" book
- Use content to develop Mini-Course by e-mail or online
- Use content to develop Homeschooling curriculum
- Use excerpts to make Quotes book
- Record reading as an audio book
- Use content as e-zine articles
- Use content for web pages along with AdSense
- Use excerpts to combine with original material for a new book
- Use excerpts along with images to create flash movies
- Use collection of PD books to create a membership site
- Use referenced authors and books to discover "new" PD materials
- Use poems or quotes to create posters

The important thing to remember here is to use your imagination...the sky is the limit. And while you're at it, I want you to think about something even more amazing—just how VAST this Public Domain treasure field really is. Are you ready for this? Try **85 million** books on every conceivable topic know to the human imagination...and that does not include art, movies, photographs, and just about every other type of media imaginable.

Okay...sorry for shocking you with that statistic. Why don't you pick yourself up off the floor...I knew that piece of information would excite you but I didn't expect you to fall over. Go ahead and brush the dust off your clothes, then go grab your brown Fedora (you know the one...the "Indy" one) and get ready for the adventure of a lifetime. You are going to LOVE this!

Bulliana Jones character drawn by Spiritpainter over at Sacred Cows Online (www.sacredcowsonline.com)

BOOK COLLECTION LINKS

The first stop on our journey into the treasure fields of the Public Domain is the Book Collection Links. This section is the largest in the book, and for good reason..remember there are over 85 million books in the Public Domain. The links represented on the following pages will lead you to tens of thousands, perhaps even hundreds of thousands of Public Domain books, all waiting for discovery. While the huge quantity of available online books should be more than enough resource material to keep you busy for a very long time, please bear in mind that all those books combined still only represent less than 5% of all the books actually in the Public Domain.

The truth is, if you took all the Public Domain books currently available online, and added them to all the Public Domain books you can find on Amazon.com, Abebooks.com, Alibris.com, Ebay.com, and the other online book sites, you would STILL only be scratching the surface of books available in the Public Domain. Perhaps you are beginning to understand now that this massive treasure field deserves your focused time and attention. Now...before you go running off into the nearly endless field of downloadable books, let me give you a few words of advice...a few points to bear in mind as you head out.

FIRST: You would be wise to determine right now the type of books you want to find. What niche markets are you working in? It is much easier to determine WHERE to search if you know WHAT you are looking for. In other words, if you want to find old books on Massage Therapy, you will not want to waste your time searching on the websites that only have classic literature. Make a list of topical keywords and keyword phrases related to your niche so that you can approach the sites with some direction and focus. Remember, since you do not know exactly what books await you, smart preparation beforehand will save you A LOT of time. It will also help you identify books for your niche more quickly. Believe me...having spent countless hours looking for those treasures, I speak from experience.

SECOND: Having actual book titles or author names related to your niche would make life even easier, wouldn't it? Well there is a great tool to help you identify those books and authors based on your keywords and keyword phrases, and I want to take a little time here to talk about it. This tool has proven invaluable to me.

Imagine having a software program that makes identifying and locating Public Domain book titles and authors easy. That is exactly what you'll find with this amazing tool. Here's how the software works...You type in your keyword(s) or keyword phrase related to your niche and click "Go." The software then begins it's search for books related to your keyword(s). The software primarily searches for related books on the AbeBooks.com website. It even provides prices and clickable links that take you directly to the books it discoveries on the Abebooks.com site. But here is what makes it so valuable...it not only identifies the books that are related to your keyword, it also checks them against the online copyright renewal databases to help you determine whether the book is actually in the Public Domain. Amazing!

Title	Author	Year (Pre 1923)	Status	Price
Aromatherapy Massage (Essential Oils for Health and Pleasure)	HARE, MARGE	1985	pre 1923	$5.38
The R.E.A. Book (Rubbing Saves Pain)	Unstated	1903	pre 1923	$8.30

Title	Author	Year (1923-1949)	Status	Price
Theory and practice of body massage (U.S. National Bureau of Standards, NBSIR 73-412)	Frank Nichols	1948	no match	$2.99
Theory and practice of body massage (U.S. National Bureau of Standards, NBSIR 73-412)	Frank Nichols	1945	no match	$2.99
Theory and practice of body massage (U.S. National Bureau of Standards, NBSIR 73-412)	Frank Nichols	1948	no match	$2.39
Our Method of Gentle Massage	Raua, Gloria, Bright Light	1948	no match	$6.00
THE COMPLETE GUIDE TO BODY CULTURE	HENDELLER, A. F.	1944	no match	$1.99
OUR METHOD OF GENTLE MASSAGE	RAUA GLORIA AND BRIGHT LIGHT	1945	no match	$5.00
TRAINING ROOM MANUAL	CRAMER, Frank	1945	no match	$8.00
ZONE REFLEX WITH DIET, MASSAGE AND HYDROTHERAPY	RILEY, JOE SHELBY & W E. DAGLISH	1942	no match	$6.00
ZONE REFLEX and DIET MASSAGE HYDROTHERAPY	RILEY and DAGLISH	1942	no match	$7.00
TABER'S DIGEST OF MEDICAL TERMS MEDICINE - SURGERY - NURSING - DIETTICS - PHYSICAL THERAPY THE COLLEGE OF SWEDISH MASSAGE	Taber, Clarence Wilbur	1935	no match	$8.00
Rohrer's Illustrated Book on Scientific Modern Beauty Culture Hair-dyeing, Bleaching, Henna, Care of the Hair and Scalp, Facial Massage, Beautifying, Neurology, Shampooing, etc.	Rohrer	1924	no match	$8.00

Title	Author	Year (1950-1962)	Status	Price
The Man and the Massage of the De Tournerod	Eds. Peter F.	1962	no match	$4.00
Franklin D Roosevelt Selected Speeches, Messages, Press conferences and Letters	Edited By Basil Rauch	1957	no match	$4.00

Then armed with your newfound titles and authors, you can choose to buy the books directly from AbeBooks, or you can head on out to the links pages to see if any of the books are available online for free. Who knows, you just might find some of them. Remember, it's more difficult find a book if you don't know the title or author. This software gives you those. Regardless of how you choose to use it though, getting this software is really a no-brainer. So before you begin going to the book sites, put your bookmark in this page, head over to the website (**www.thepublicdomainexpert.com/explorer**) and pick up your own copy of the software...we'll wait for you to return. Okay, do you have it now? Good job!

THIRD: If you're like me, you might also want to just spend time browsing through the titles listed on the websites. It's kind of like rummaging around in one of those old used bookstores...something I love to do. Nothing beats the feeling of finding that nugget while searching through page after page of books. Searching by keyword IS quicker, and using the software above can make your exploration lightning fast. Sometimes, it is okay to just relax and have fun with it. Sure...the object of the hunt is to find those treasures...and time IS money...but also remember that there is joy in the journey.

FOURTH: There is just one last thing to take care of before you get started. This treasure hunt can be extremely addicting, and before you know it, hours will have passed. So before you travel to the next section and begin your search, you will want to prepare yourself for the journey by following these important treasure hunting steps:

1. **Go to the bathroom.** You're going to be glued to your computer for a while so why torture yourself. Just go get it over with. You'll thank me later.

2. **Put on some comfy clothes.** Hey, you might as well be comfortable, right?

3. **Get a sandwich and your favorite beverage.** You don't really need this but...okay, so you do really need it...sorry. (While you're at it, eat a candy bar for me!)

4. **Get a notepad and pen.** If you're like me, you will not remember everything you discover as you head down those rabbit trails...and yes...you will find rabbit trails. You might even find a rabbit hole or two. But just how far down the rabbit hole are you willing to go? Just ask Alice...she's in the Public Domain!

5. **Fire up your iPod** with some good tunes or the latest teleseminar. You CAN multi-task, right?

Finally, as you begin to work through the Code Book, you will notice that I have provided screenshots of some of the sites along with some additional comments on items to check out while you are on the site. Pay attention to these. They are provided to help you maximize your visit to those sites. Also, I provided a section for each site to add your own comments. Some of these sites will not fit what you're looking for. Others may become a goldmine for you. So make sure you take notes. That way you don't have to wonder which site was the one where you saw that book you wanted.

6. **Turn the page** and GO FIND SOME BOOKS! I'm happy for you...you're going to have a blast!

"There is more treasure in books than in all the pirates' loot on Treasure Island... and best of all, you can enjoy these riches every day of your life." —Walt Disney

19th Century Schoolbooks

http://digital.library.pitt.edu/nietz/

The Nietz Old Textbook Collection is one of several well-known collections of 19th Century schoolbooks in the United States. Examine digital editions of 140 schoolbooks and two surveys of historic schoolbooks by John Nietz, the founder of the Nietz Old Textbook Collection. The online collection contains page images as well as searchable text.

Comments / Notes: _____

_____

_____

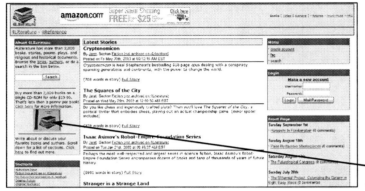

4Literature

http://www.4literature.net/

4Literature is a web site devoted to the reading, writing, and discussion of literature. 4Literature has more than 2,000 books, stories, poems, plays, and religious and historical documents that can be read online.

Save yourself some time and effort—buy the CD!

Comments / Notes: _____

_____

_____

_____

African American Texts

http://etext.virginia.edu/subjects/African-American.html

The Etext Center mission is as follows: To create an on-line archive of standards-based texts and images in the humanities; and to build and support user communities adept at the creation and use of online resources. The emphasis in this collection is African-American texts.

Comments / Notes: _____

_____

_____

_____

Alex Catalogue of Electronic Texts

http://www.infomotions.com/alex2/

The Alex Catalogue of Electronic Texts is a full-text indexed collection of classic American and English literature as well as Western philosophy in the public domain and written or translated into English.

Comments / Notes: _____

_____

_____

_____

Athena

http://un2sg4.unige.ch/athena/html/athome.html

Athena endeavors to provide the Internet users with good educational texts, useful databases, accurate information and valuable links. Thus there are many of megabytes of files.

Comments / Notes: _____
_____
_____

Authorama

http://www.authorama.com/

Authorama features completely free books from a variety of different authors, collected here for you to read online or offline.

Comments / Notes: _____
_____
_____

Avalon Project

http://www.yale.edu/lawweb/avalon/avalon.htm

The Avalon Project is dedicated to providing access to primary source materials in the fields of Law, History, Economics, Politics, Diplomacy and Government.

Comments / Notes: _____
_____
_____

Bibliographical Society of America

http://www.bibsocamer.org/BibSite/contents.htm

A major collection of biographical resources from the Biographical Society of America.

Comments / Notes: _____
_____
_____

Bibliomania

http://www.bibliomania.com/

Free Online Literature with more than 2000 Classic Texts, Literature Book Notes, Author Biographies, Book Summaries and Reference Book. Read Classic Fiction, Drama, Poetry, Short Stories and Contemporary Articles and Interviews. Research Reference Books, Dictionaries, Quotations, Classic Non-fiction, Biographies and Religious Texts.

Comments / Notes: _____
_____
_____

Books About California History and Culture

http://www.books-about-california.com/

This web site is a personal library of public domain e-texts and pictures about California and the old West. Also included are lists of books by California Publishers, and a list of books about California.

Comments / Notes: _____

_____

_____

_____

Books on Demand

http://www.lib.umi.com/bod/

Nearly 150,000 out-of-print books are at your fingertips with this Web-based program. Their vaults contain thousands and thousands of copyright-cleared books, ready for black-and-white reproduction the minute you place your order.

Comments / Notes: _____

_____

_____

_____

BookRags: 3,500 Literature Summaries & 70,000 Topic Guides

http://www.bookrags.com/

BookRags is an accumulation of comprehensive guides to classical literature, published for free on BookRags.com.

Comments / Notes: _____

_____

_____

_____

Bralyn E-Text Archive

http://www.bralyn.net/etext/

There is an enormous collection of E-Text located here. All the text is indexed nightly and work is underway to make the texts fully searchable! The texts are mostly public domain and cover nearly every topic including Poetry, History, Social Sciences, Humor and Culture.

The Directory Tree is probably the quickest way around here.

Comments / Notes: _____

_____

_____

_____

Brookings Institution Press

http://brookings.nap.edu/

The Books Online program provides online access to full-text versions of a large and growing list of titles. Now you can browse and search over 30,000 pages of cutting-edge public policy research from your computer, and print selected pages one at a time.

Comments / Notes: _____

_____

_____

CELT: Corpus of Electronic Texts

http://www.ucc.ie/celt/

CELT, the Corpus of Electronic Texts, brings the wealth of Irish literary and historical culture to the Internet, for the use and benefit of everyone worldwide. It has a searchable online database consisting of contemporary and historical texts from many areas, including literature and the other arts.

Comments / Notes: _____

_____

_____

Chinese Text Initiative

http://etext.lib.virginia.edu/chinese/

Chinese Text Initiative, an effort to make texts of Chinese literature available on the World Wide Web. These sites are still very much under construction and we have not yet finished final copy-editing.

Comments / Notes: _____

_____

_____

_____

Don't overlook the audio books!

Christian Classics Ethereal Library

http://www.ccel.org/

Classic Christian books in electronic format, selected for your edification. There is enough good reading material here to last you a lifetime, if you give each work the time it deserves! All of the books on this server are believed to be in the public domain in the United States unless otherwise specified. Copy them freely for any purpose. Outside of the US, check your local copyright laws.

Comments / Notes: _____

_____

_____

_____

Classic Bookshelf

http://www.classicbookshelf.com/
You'll find classic literature here for free.

Comments / Notes: _____
_____
_____

Classic Herbal Texts

http://www.henriettesherbal.com/
Herbal medicine and culinary herbs: one of the oldest and largest herbal information sites on the net.

Many classic herbal texts here...also, much of the site is now on CD.

Comments / Notes: _____
_____
_____

Classical Authors Directory

http://authorsdirectory.com/index.shtml
Classical Authors, Children's Books & Stories for Children with Poetry Fables & Fairy Tales and more.

Comments / Notes: _____
_____
_____

Classic Reader

http://www.classicreader.com/
Classic Reader offers a large collection of free classic books by authors such as Dickens, Austen, Shakespeare and many others.

Comments / Notes: _____
_____
_____

Classics in the History of Psychology

http://psychclassics.yorku.ca/topic.htm
Classics in the History of Psychology is an effort to make the full texts of a large number of historically significant public domain documents on the World Wide Web.

Comments / Notes: _____
_____
_____

Complete Works of William Shakespeare

http://www.shakespeare-literature.com/
The title says it all…this site is a resource for both students and Shakespeare fanatics.

Comments / Notes: _____
_____
_____

Early Canadiana Online

http://www.canadiana.org/eco/english/index.html
Early Canadiana Online (ECO) is a digital library providing access to 2,076,137 pages of Canada's printed heritage. It features works published from the time of the first European settlers up to the early 20th Century.

Comments / Notes: _____
_____
_____

Earthly Pursuits: Old Book Library

http://www.earthlypursuits.com/Books/OldBooklibrary.htm
Earthly Pursuits features a collection of Public Domain books including the topics of gardening, botany, agriculture, horticulture, floriculture, the language of flowers, bibliomania, food, life and other earthly things.

Comments / Notes: _____
_____
_____

Easy Media Broadcast

http://www.easymediabroadcast.com/
A collection of e-books that include titles from classic literature, as well as titles from children's and esoteric literature. They also include a number of foreign language and audio books.

Comments / Notes: _____
_____
_____

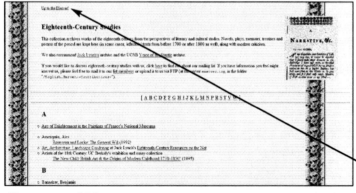

Eighteenth-Century Studies

http://eserver.org/18th/
This collection archives works of the eighteenth century from the perspectives of literary and cultural studies, including novels, plays, memoirs, treatises and poems.

There are a lot of great links here. Also, make sure to check out this link! It will take you to some more goodies!

Comments / Notes: _____
_____
_____

Eldritch Press

http://www.eldritchpress.org/

Everything at this site has now been placed in the public domain with a Creative Commons deed (except two or three pieces copyrighted by others and used by permission).

Comments / Notes: _____

_____

_____

Electronic Nautical Books

http://www.boat-links.com/books/electron.html

Public Domain book resource with a specific focus on nautical books.

Comments / Notes: _____

_____

_____

Electronic Text Center

http://etext.lib.virginia.edu/

The Etext Center mission is to create an online archive of standards-based texts and images in the humanities; and to build and support user communities adept at the creation and use of online resources.

Definitely check out the offline collections as well. There are some gems worth mining here.

Comments / Notes: _____

_____

_____

Ex-Classics Web Site

http://www.exclassics.com/

This web site is dedicated to rescuing "ex-classic" works from obscurity and making them available online, both for reading directly, and for downloading.

Comments / Notes: _____

_____

_____

Fly Fishing History

http://www.flyfishinghistory.com/bibliography.htm

Hey all you fishermen, here is a bibliography of fly fishing books, nearly all of which are in the public domain!

Comments / Notes: _____

_____

_____

Forum Romanum

http://www.forumromanum.org/index2.html

Forum Romanum is a collaborative project among scholars, teachers, and students with the broad purpose of bringing classical literature out of college libraries and into a more accessible, online medium. Toward this end, we host a number of materials for students of the classical world, including texts, translations, and other pedagogical resources.

Comments / Notes: _____

_____

_____

_____

Free Library

http://www.thefreelibrary.com/

A website of classic books by famous authors, all of which are in the public domain.

Comments / Notes: _____

_____

_____

_____

FPD: Free Public Domain

http://fpd.iwarp.com/

This site presently lists hundreds of Public Domain Fairy Tales from The Brothers Grimm Fairy Tales, Hans Christian Anderson Fairy Tales, Arabian Nights Entertainments, Blue Fairy Book, Crimson Fairy Book, Red Fairy Book, Violet Fairy Book, and the Yellow Fairy Book.

Comments / Notes: _____

_____

_____

_____

Free Self-Help Books

http://www.absolute1.net/free_self_help_books_online.html

Find a growing number of motivational books to help you to experience healing, self esteem, complete prosperity, abundant success, & financial freedom.

There are a number of excellent links at the bottom of this page in addition to the onsite books.

Comments / Notes: _____

_____

_____

_____

History of Science Bibliography

http://web.uflib.ufl.edu/spec/rarebook/science/

The George A. Smathers Libraries' Rare Book Collection is rich in a variety of rare and special books, including books that are of interest to scholars of natural history, history of science, botanical books, and other subjects.

Comments / Notes: _____

_____

_____

_____

HTI Public Domain Modern English Collection

http://www.hti.umich.edu/p/pd-modeng/

A collection of Modern English texts in the Public Domain. The texts in this collection come from a variety of sources on the Internet, including the Oxford Text Archive, Project Gutenberg, the Online Book Initiative, and contributions from individual text encoders.

Comments / Notes: _____

_____

_____

_____

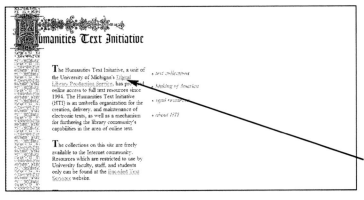

Humanities Text Initiative

http://www.hti.umich.edu/

The Humanities Text Initiative is a unit of the University of Michigan's Digital Library Production Service and oversees the creation, delivery, and maintenance of electronic texts.

Also check out this link, then click on "Collections." it will show you more "public" and "restricted" resources that are available!

Comments / Notes: _____

_____

_____

_____

Humanist Texts

http://www.humanistictexts.org/

Multicultural extracts that portray the wit, wisdom, and poetry of individuals as they reflect on ethics, philosophy, knowledge, and human relationships.

Comments / Notes: _____

_____

_____

_____

Hypertexts (American Studies)

http://xroads.virginia.edu/~HYPER/hypertex.html

Electronic texts for the study of American culture.

Comments / Notes: _____
_____
_____
_____

Indiana University LRTRS

http://www.letrs.indiana.edu/online_rw.html

The Library Electronic Text Resource Service (LETRS) provides humanities-related electronic texts via the Internet through a number of excellent links and resources.

Comments / Notes: _____
_____
_____
_____

International Children's Library

http://www.icdlbooks.org/books/index.html

The International Children's Digital Library (ICDL) is a research project to create a digital library of outstanding children's books from all over the world.

Comments / Notes: _____
_____
_____
_____

Internet Archive

http://www.archive.org/

The Internet Archive is an 'Internet library,' with the purpose of offering permanent access for researchers, historians, and scholars to historical collections that exist in digital format.

Notice the RSS feeds for those of you who need content for your niche sites. There are many, many gems on this site...take time to look around.

Comments / Notes: _____
_____
_____
_____

Internet Archive of Texts and Documents (Hanover College)

http://history.hanover.edu/texts.html

The principal goal of the *Internet Archive of Texts and Documents*, a creation of faculty and students in the History Department of Hanover College, is to make primary texts and secondary sources on the internet available to students and faculty for use in history and humanity classes.

Comments / Notes: _____

_____

_____

_____

Internet Classics Archive

http://classics.mit.edu/

Bringing the wisdom of the classics to the Internet since 1994. A collection of over 400 classic literature texts by nearly 60 authors.

Comments / Notes: _____

_____

_____

_____

Internet Library of Early Journals

http://www.bodley.ox.ac.uk/ilej/

ILEJ, the "Internet Library of Early Journals" offers digitized runs of 18th and 19th century journals, and makes these images available on the Internet, together with their associated bibliographic data.

Comments / Notes: _____

_____

_____

_____

Internet Medieval Sourcebook

http://www.fordham.edu/halsall/sbook.html
A selection of texts from the Medieval period of history.

Also explore the links to "Ancient History Sourcebook" and "Modern History Sourcebook" for many more Public Domain resources.

Comments / Notes: _____

_____

_____

_____

Internet Public Library

http://www.ipl.org/div/subject/browse/hum60.60.00/

The Internet Public Library has an excellent collection of links to online texts and texts collections.

Comments / Notes: _____

_____

_____

_____

Knowledge Rush

http://www.knowledgerush.com/Books.htm

Knowledge Rush lives up to its name…they have a massive collection of books listed in alphabetical order by title.

Do not overlook researching the "Encyclopedia" section. I found a lot of helpful and useful information here.

Comments / Notes: _____

_____

_____

Kurt Stüber's Online Library

http://www.biolib.de/

This site (offered in both English and German) specializes in classic texts that focus on the various areas of Biological Science.

Comments / Notes: _____

_____

_____

_____

_____

Library of Southern Literature

http://docsouth.unc.edu/southlit/index.html

The "Library of Southern Literature" includes a wide range of literary works of the American South published before 1924and includes some of the earliest texts about America written by British discoverers.

Comments / Notes: _____

_____

_____

_____

_____

Literature for Children

http://palmm.fcla.edu/juv/

Literature for Children is a collection of some of the best writings of children's literature that have been published in the United States and Great Britain from the early 1800's and later.

Comments / Notes: _____

_____

_____

Literature Network

http://www.online-literature.com/

The Literature Network offers searchable online literature for the student, educator, or enthusiast. They currently have over 1200 full books and over 2000 short stories and poems by over 250 authors.

There are also over 8,500 quotes here to use in your Public Domain or Information products.

Comments / Notes: _____

_____

_____

Literature Project

http://www.literatureproject.com/

Literature Project is a collection of classic books, poems, speeches, and plays.

Comments / Notes: _____

_____

_____

Litrix Reading Room

http://www.litrix.com/

A collection of classic literature writings from several areas of focus including Science Fiction and Mystery.

Comments / Notes: _____

_____

_____

Luminarium

http://www.luminarium.org/lumina.htm

The Luminarium Anthology covers Middle, Renaissance and Seventeenth Century English Literature. Very well-organized.

Comments / Notes: _____

_____

_____

Mad Cybrarian's Library

http://www.fortunecity.com/victorian/richmond/88/index.html
A huge collection of books organized alphabetically by author's last name.

Comments / Notes: _____
_____
_____
_____

Making of America Digital Library

http://www.hti.umich.edu/m/moagrp/
Making of America is a digital library of primary sources in American social history, with special attention to the subject areas of education, psychology, American history, sociology, religion, and science and technology and contains approximately 9,500 books and 50,000 journal articles from the 19th century.

Comments / Notes: _____
_____
_____
_____

Million Book Project

http://www.archive.org/details/millionbooks
The goal of The Million Book Project is to digitize a million books by 2005...you know what that means...lots of books to dig through!

Pay attention to what is listed in these sections. It will provide you with some clues as to what people are looking for.

Comments / Notes: _____
_____
_____

Missouri Botanical Garden Library

http://www.illustratedgarden.org/mobot/rarebooks/
The Missouri Botanical Garden Library has digitized and preserved beautifully illustrated botanically books from their private holdings in order to make them available to an international audience.

Comments / Notes: _____
_____
_____
_____
_____

New Thought Library

http://newthoughtlibrary.com/new.htm
Provides a comprehensive online library that archives all public domain New Thought works in multiple medias.

Grab the latest New Thought book additions right here...and do not forget the wealth of other titles as well.

Comments / Notes: _____
_____
_____
_____

Online Literature Library

http://www.literature.org/authors/
A collection of classic literature listed by author.

Comments / Notes: _____
_____
_____
_____

Online Medieval and Classical Library

http://sunsite.berkeley.edu/OMACL/
The Online Medieval and Classical Library (OMACL) is a collection of some of the most important literary works of Classical and Medieval civilization.

Comments / Notes: _____
_____
_____
_____

Oxford Text Archive

http://ota.ahds.ac.uk/
The Oxford Text Archive Website works closely with members of the Arts and Humanities academic community to collect, catalogue, and preserve high-quality electronic texts for research and teaching. The OTA currently distributes more than 2500 resources in over 25 different languages.

Comments / Notes: _____
_____
_____
_____

Page By Page Books

http://www.pagebypagebooks.com/

Page by Page books is committed to bringing you a wide selection of the best public domain books available, all in an easy to read format.

Comments / Notes: _____
_____
_____

Perseus Digital Library

http://www.perseus.tufts.edu/

Perseus is an evolving digital library whose primary goal is to bring a wide range of source materials to as large an audience as possible.

Comments / Notes: _____
_____
_____

Project Gutenberg

http://www.gutenberg.org/catalog/

Project Gutenberg is the oldest producer of free ebooks on the Internet. This is the place to start your search. They have over 17,000 free books in their catalog.

Enjoy Project Gutenberg's excellent searching tools which allow you to search in the ways that you prefer the most...by browsing or by keyword.

Comments / Notes: _____
_____
_____

Project Gutenberg of Australia

http://gutenberg.net.au/plusfifty.html

Works provided by Project Gutenberg of Australia which are in the public domain in Australia.

Comments / Notes: _____
_____
_____

Rare Books...Rare Manuscripts

http://www.fjg.com/rare/default.htm

A real nice collection of links to sites containing rare books and manuscripts.

Comments / Notes: _____
_____
_____

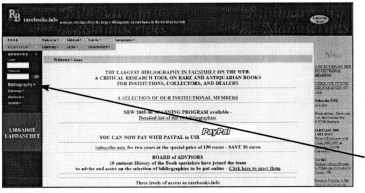

RareBooks.Info

http://www.rarebooks.info

This site features the largest bibliography of rare books in facsimile in the world.

You have to pay to search the bibliography pages, but then you DO get access to 600,000 pages of bibliographies, with 20,000 more being added every month. That is a lot of research power!

Comments / Notes: _____

_____

_____

_____

Read Print

http://www.readprint.com/

The Read Print website offers thousands of free books for students, teachers, and the classic enthusiast. Listed by author.

Comments / Notes: _____

_____

_____

_____

Religious and Sacred Texts

http://davidwiley.com/religion.html

This site hosts a broad variety of religious texts, from the Bhagavad Gita and Bible to Zen texts…and all points in between.

Comments / Notes: _____

_____

_____

_____

Renascence Editions

http://www.uoregon.edu/~rbear/ren.htm

An online repository of works printed in English between the years 1477 and 1799.

Comments / Notes: _____

_____

_____

_____

Rosetta Project

http://www.editec.net/

The Rosetta Project is the largest collection of illustrated antique children's books available online.

Comments / Notes: _____

_____

_____

Sacred Text Archive

http://www.sacred-texts.com/index.htm

This site is a freely available archive of electronic texts about religion, mythology, legends and folklore, and occult and esoteric topics.

Get 1,000 of their most popular Public Domain books on CD for only $49.95. You get great books and help them continue making these treasures available.

Comments / Notes: _____

_____

_____

Universal Library

http://tera-3.ul.cs.cmu.edu/

A significant collection of literary, artistic, and scientific works that has been digitally preserved and made freely available for our education, study, and appreciation.

Comments / Notes: _____

_____

_____

University of Toronto English Library

http://www.library.utoronto.ca/utel/

University of Toronto English Library collection of poetry and prose featuring over 350 authors.

Comments / Notes: _____

_____

_____

University of Virginia: Early American Fiction

http://etext.lib.virginia.edu/eaf/pubindex.html

The Early American Fiction collection includes 886 volumes American fiction dating from 1789-1875.

Comments / Notes: _____

_____

_____

Victorian Web

http://www.victorianweb.org/

Literature, history and culture from the Victorian age.

Comments / Notes: _____

_____

_____

_____

Victorian Women Writer's Project

http://www.indiana.edu/~letrs/vwwp/index.html

The goal of the Victorian Women Writers Project is to produce highly accurate transcriptions of works by British women writers of the 19th century.

Comments / Notes: _____

_____

_____

_____

Wiretap

http://wiretap.area.com/Gopher/Library/Classic/

A Gopher index collection of classic texts.

Comments / Notes: _____

_____

_____

_____

World eBook Library

http://worldebooklibrary.com/index.html

This massive collection boasts the world's largest digital archive of PDF eBooks and eDocuments, hosting more than 250,000+ PDF eBooks and eDocuments.

They offer public access to some of their collection, but members have access to more than 250,000 books...for only $8.95 per year! Spend the money.

Comments / Notes: _____

_____

_____

_____

World Literature Author

http://www.litfix.com/

Purchase and research world literature titles in the Public Domain. Buy the book, read it for free online or download it as an audio book.

Comments / Notes: _____

_____

_____

_____

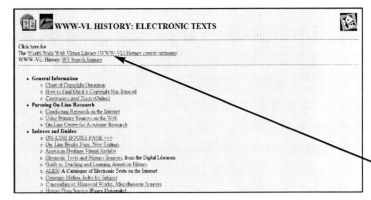

WWW Virtual Library

http://vlib.iue.it/history/materials/e-texts.html

A large collection of links to indexes, repositories and specific languages.

Get out your Public Domain shovels and start digging...and while you're at it, be sure to check out this link as well.

Comments / Notes: _____

_____

_____

_____

Write in your new Public Domain Book Collection link discoveries here:

Write in your new Public Domain Book Collection link discoveries here:

_____

_____

_____

_____

_____

_____

_____

_____

_____

_____

_____

_____

_____

_____

_____

_____

_____

_____

_____

_____

_____

_____

_____

_____

_____

_____

PUBLISHER LINKS

The Publisher Links section will be an important part of your Public Domain research. While you will not find books or other resources to download for free on these sites, the information they offer may be even more valuable in some cases. Here is what to look for as you visit these pages:

1. Take a look at the products they are selling. Many of these are based on Public Domain resources, and in some cases, might even be exact reprints. The products they offer will give you a good idea of just what is available...think about it...there is a reason why THEY are selling it, right?! And it certainly aids in your quest to have actual titles for the books that fit your niche.

2. Pay attention to the information they offer about the books or products they are selling. This is the same information you can use to locate your own copy. Often they will include the title, author, year of original publication and more. Take that information and head over to Abebooks or Alibris and search for the book there. Or you can even plug the info into your favorite search engine. Who knows, the book may turn up being online. But since it is hard to locate a book you don't know exists, don't be afraid to dig around. Remember, there are 85 million Public Domain books out there.

3. Use these resources as a bibliography to discover obscure titles by authors that are perhaps not listed anywhere else. I found a complete listing of titles for one of my favorite authors on one of these sites, and it was the only place that listed some of the titles. I then used their list as a checklist to find what I was looking for on Ebay, Abebooks and used bookstores.

4. In some cases, the books produced are exact reprints, meaning the pages are scanned from an original book and printed exactly, and as such, are still in the Public Domain. What is so great about this is that you can purchase a copy of the book from the publisher, scan it yourself (or have it typed), run it through OCR software and you have your e-book. This is especially helpful when the original for the book you want is selling for hundreds of dollars. I have used this exact strategy with great results!

5. You can discover excellent resources for images, documentaries and movies. Most CD's or DVD's you purchase from a publisher WILL be protected by license. BUT (and this is a BIG but), they had to get their source material from somewhere! Very often, they found it online. Again...you cannot find something if you do not know to look for it. I have located many of the source material websites these guys are using for their own products. I've included all those links in this Code Book, so have fun! Go create your own products.

6. Many of these publishers offer their books through Amazon.com. Find a title you are interested in on one of these sites, then go to Amazon.com and do a title search for it. Check the book's Amazon.com Sales Ranking to get an idea of whether there is interest in that title or author. A focused search on Amazon.com can also show you if others are publishing the same title. Don't forget to do an author search while you're there. You may find even more books by the author, or related titles that are also into the Public Domain.

Whatever you do, do NOT underestimate the value of this section. Many of my greatest Public Domain discoveries were made on some of these sites. So take time and get to know them...research them. You just might strike gold!

A2ZCDS

http://www.a2zcds.com/

A2ZCDS is the world's largest and fastest growing innovative multi-media library. Through its vast and unique distribution network, the company provides historical and educational CDs and DVDs covering thousands of topics to every corner of the globe.

Comments / Notes: _____

_____

_____

Ayer Company Publishers

http://ayerpub.com/CategoryPage.asp

Ayer Company Publishers is a reprint publisher of rare and hard to find titles with topics ranging from the civil war to aviation

— Search titles by browsing categories or by keyword.

Comments / Notes: _____

_____

_____

_____

B & R Samizdat Express

http://store.yahoo.com/samizdat/

The B&R Samizdat Express is a small book publishing company which sells public domain texts on PC diskettes (mainly classic works of literature and government documents).

Comments / Notes: _____

_____

_____

_____

Bartleby

http://www.bartleby.com/

The preeminent Internet publisher of literature, reference and verse providing students, researchers and the intellectually curios with unlimited access to books and information on the web, free of charge.

Comments / Notes: _____

_____

_____

_____

Cornerstone Books

http://cornerstone.wwwhubs.com/framepage.htm

A non-profit site dedicated to providing free access to some of the very best inspirational/self-improvement books ever written. Featuring the full texts of over 100 complete books available to read free online! A great reference resource as well.

Comments / Notes: _____

_____

_____

Cyder Press

http://www.cyderpress.co.uk/

The Cyder Press is a small press that reprints long out-of-print or little-known works by the Dymock Poets themselves, and by other writers with cognate regional, literary or period connections. Each volume is introduced by a contemporary scholar.

Comments / Notes: _____

_____

_____

Donald G. Carty

http://www.lulu.com/donaldcarty

Donald Gordon Carty, is an internationally known author, personal training and development consultant, motivational speaker, and the president of the Personal Development Institute. His site contains many classic Public Domain books.

Comments / Notes: _____

_____

_____

Dover Publications

http://www.doverpublications.com/

Dover Publications has built their reputation by offering remarkable products at amazing prices. They primarily publish books no longer published by their original publishers—often, but not always, books in the public domain. Over 8,000 titles.

Take advantage of Dover's collection of catalogs.

Comments / Notes: _____

_____

_____

_____

Erskine Press: Archival Facsimiles Limited

http://www.erskine-press.com/

The Erskine Press publishes unusual and interesting books covering a wide range of interests. Twice a year it produces books dealing with the HEROIC AGE OF ANTARCTIC EXPLORATION, covering facsimiles of diaries dealing with, for example, the ill-fated Scott expedition; new diaries and previously unpublished works, as well as first English translations of European expeditions of the late 19th and early 20th centuries.

Comments / Notes: _____

_____

_____

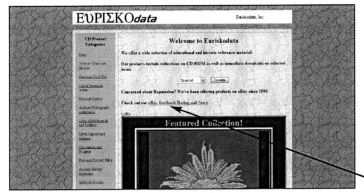

Euriskodata

http://www.euriskodata.com/

Euriskodata offers a wide selection of educational and historic reference material. Their products include collections on CD-ROM as well as immediate downloads on selected items.

Make sure you check out their Ebay store as well.

Comments / Notes: _____

_____

_____

Facsimile 19th Century Books and Publications

http://www.vintagevolumes.com/oldbooks.html

Offers reproductions of Victorian / Civil War era books.

Comments / Notes: _____

_____

_____

Food Books

http://www.foodbooks.com/facsimil.htm

Now you can own an exact replica of authentic American and British classic cookbooks. They are better than the original because they are printed on acid-free paper, contain scholarly introductions, glossaries and indexes. Originals of some of these books are so prohibitively expensive only museums can own them.

Comments / Notes: _____

_____

_____

_____

Good Old Days

http://www.goodolddaysonline.com/

The website for the popular magazine of the "Good Old Days!" Good Old Days® and Good Old Days® Specials are published monthly (Good Old Days®) and bi-monthly (Good Old Days® Specials) by House of White Birches.

Comments / Notes: _____

_____

_____

Gustav's Library Publishing

http://www.gustavslibrary.com/

Gustav's Library Publishing was established to provide today's reading public with quality reprints of vintage American rare books. The authors and publishing houses represented here include many of the lesser known, yet highly influential, contributors.

Comments / Notes: _____

_____

_____

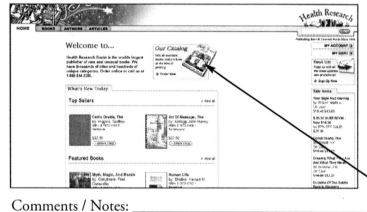

Health Research Books

http://www.healthresearchbooks.com/index.php

Health Research Books has been proud to offer a stunning array of these rare and unusual books since 1952. Their vision and purpose have remained the same throughout these past 50 years: Keep this information available to the citizens of the world!

You definitely want their catalog!

Comments / Notes: _____

_____

_____

_____

Hidden Knowledge

http://www.hidden-knowledge.com/

Hidden Knowledge publishes new books, never published before, and they re-publish old books that you can't find anywhere else in six different electronic formats.

Comments / Notes: _____

_____

_____

_____

Higginson Book Company

http://www.higginsonbooks.com/index.html

Higginson Book Company offers an unparalleled collection of American Family History reprints, now available for genealogical research! They have been offering the genealogical community more than 15,000 quality book and map reprints since 1965.

Comments / Notes: _____
_____
_____

Historical Text Archive

http://historicaltextarchive.com/

The Historical Text Archive publishes high quality articles, books, essays, documents, historical photos, and links for a broad range of historical subjects.

Comments / Notes: _____
_____
_____

Horizon Books

http://www.horizonbook.com/

Horizon Books is operated as a mail order business and a Web store, specializing in books on Travel & Exploration, Natural History, Plant Hunting and Gardening.

Comments / Notes: _____
_____
_____
_____

Be sure you read this notice, then have fun digging.

Kessinger Publishing

http://www.kessinger.net/index.php

Kessinger Publishing utilizes advanced technology to publish and preserve thousands of rare, scarce, and out-of-print books. They produce a vast collection of books from the Public Domain.

Comments / Notes: _____
_____
_____
_____

L & S Trading

http://www.luckowgroup.com/l&sbooks.htm

The Luckow Group publishes books pertaining to the Stock Market that are from the Public Domain.

Comments / Notes: _____
_____
_____

McGowan Book Company

http://www.mcgowanbooks.com/catalog.html

Booksellers that specialize in used and rare books including a great collection on Abraham Lincoln and The American Civil War.

Comments / Notes: _____
_____
_____

Metaphysical Concepts

http://www.metaphysical-concepts.com

Metaphysical Concepts publishes books on alternative medicine, natural cures, metaphysics and more, many of which are from the Public Domain.

Comments / Notes: _____
_____
_____

PaleoPublications

http://www.paleopubs.com/

PaleoPublications specializes in antique, rare, and used works related to the natural sciences.

Comments / Notes: _____
_____
_____

Paperless Archives (Secret and historical documents, recordings, photos, etc.)

http://www.paperlessarchives.com/index.html

Provides access to once secret and historical documents, recordings, photos, video and audio.

For some valuable information on how to use the Freedom of Information Act to obtain "secret" documents, click here and then choose the FAQ section.

Comments / Notes: _____
_____
_____

Rare Books about Static Electricity, Lightning, Wireless, and Radio.

http://people.clarityconnect.com/webpages2/arcsandsparks/reprintpage.html

Sells reprint books from the Public Domain about static electricity, lightning, wireless, and radio.

Comments / Notes: _____

_____

_____

Rare Christian Books

http://www.rarechristianbooks.com/

Rare Christian books provides just that…rare Christian books. The books are not available onsite but they do provide titles and authors so that you can locate them through other sources.

Comments / Notes: _____

_____

_____

RDMc Publishing

http://www.rdmc.net

RDMc Publishing publishes reprints and reproductions of rare and out-of-print books; mostly religious titles.

Comments / Notes: _____

_____

_____

Seek Publishing

http://www.seekpublishing.com/IE/index.htm

Publishers of the "Remember When?" books and other nostalgic products based on Public Domain materials.

Comments / Notes: _____

_____

_____

Soil and Health Library

http://www.soilandhealth.org/

This is a specialist library about holistic agriculture, holistic health and self-sufficient homestead living. Most of the titles in this library are out of print. Many are quite hard to find.

Click on the "Library" links to find the books. You will have to read their copyright info first to check out the books. But there are some real gems here.

Comments / Notes: _____

_____

_____

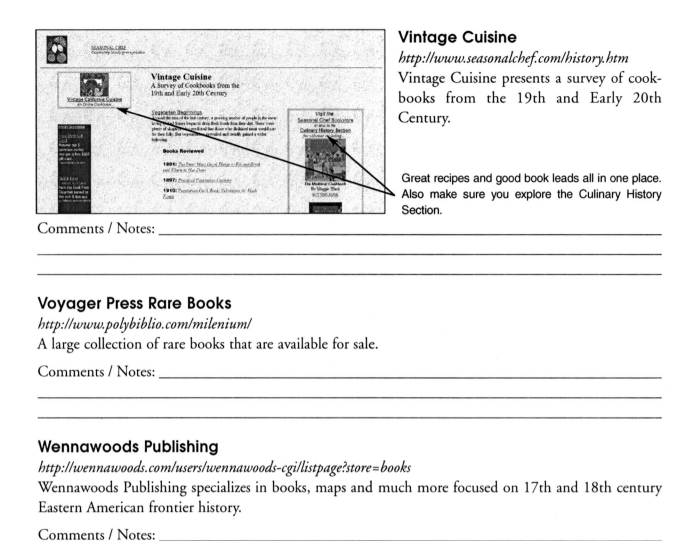

Vintage Cuisine

http://www.seasonalchef.com/history.htm

Vintage Cuisine presents a survey of cookbooks from the 19th and Early 20th Century.

Great recipes and good book leads all in one place. Also make sure you explore the Culinary History Section.

Comments / Notes: _____

_____

_____

Voyager Press Rare Books

http://www.polybiblio.com/milenium/

A large collection of rare books that are available for sale.

Comments / Notes: _____

_____

_____

Wennawoods Publishing

http://wennawoods.com/users/wennawoods-cgi/listpage?store=books

Wennawoods Publishing specializes in books, maps and much more focused on 17th and 18th century Eastern American frontier history.

Comments / Notes: _____

_____

_____

Write in your new Public Domain Publisher link discoveries here:

_____

_____

_____

_____

_____

_____

_____

_____

_____

_____

_____

_____

_____

_____

_____

_____

_____

_____

_____

_____

_____

_____

_____

_____

_____

_____

_____

_____

Write in your new Public Domain Publisher link discoveries here:

_____

_____

_____

_____

_____

_____

_____

_____

_____

_____

_____

_____

_____

_____

_____

_____

_____

_____

_____

_____

_____

_____

_____

_____

_____

_____

_____

BOOKSELLER LINKS

※

Y ou are going to spend a lot of time on these sites if you are interested in buying books. But with so many millions of books out there, it can be a nightmare to find what you are looking for...especially if you don't know the title or author. There are some great search techniques that will help you filter through all the books you don't want so that you can focus in on the ones you do want...the Public Domain books.

My favorite bookseller in this section would have to be Abebooks.com. They are one of the largest websites when it comes to searching for used books, with listings from over 13,500 book dealers selling over 80 million books. Their listings are so massive that, if you cannot locate a book on their site, chances are that it will not be listed on ANY site.

There are a number of ways to effectively use the Abebooks.com website to uncover Public Domain books. One way that we've already discussed in another section of this book is to use the powerful software, Public Domain Explorer (www.thepublicdomainexpert.com/explorer). This software's search engine actually references the listings on Abebooks.com and provides you with clickable links that take you right to the book you are interested in. I cannot stress enough how valuable this software is.

Apart from using the software, there are also some sneaky ways to filter through all those myriads of books to find those Public Domain gems. I will walk you through the process. To begin, launch your web browser and go to the Abebooks.com website. You will see a typical search tool. If you know the title or author, you can just type it in and click on "Find Book." The site will provide you with books that fit your search terms. But chances are you will NOT know the title or author, so the most effective type of search you can do is to use keywords. But also remember that we want to locate books that are in the Public Domain. Just using a keyword alone could land you thousands of book entries that are completely useless to you. You'll lose a lot of time trying to file through them all.

To narrow down your search, try this: Click on the "Advanced Search" link. You will notice that you are provided additional search parameters along with the ones from the basic search. The parameter we are most interested in is the section that allows us to define the "Published Date." This is where we will be able to narrow the search to the books only found within the years of Public Domain availability.

You will notice in the screen image here that I have entered "1700" for the "min" value and "1922" for the "max" value. I chose "1700" just because it is an arbitrary low year...the goal being to get every listing before and including 1922. Of course, I chose "1922" as the max value because we know that every book published before 1923 is definitely in the Public Domain. Once you have set these parameters, type in your keyword and click "Find Book" to get your results. Now, EVERY book that comes up is in the Public Domain, with perhaps only a few exceptions that might have been published in another country. Now another trick I usually do at this stage of the search is to sort the results so that the highest prices are shown first. This is a great way to identify some of the more difficult to locate books within your niche. It can also help you identify, relatively quickly, some titles that may be the most ideal to republish or repurpose.

Once you find a couple titles or authors that interest you in the higher priced listings, use that information to perform a new search. You may be fortunate enough to find the same book or author listed at a lower price. You may also want to consider using Google to perform a item-specific search. Who knows, you may find that expensive title online. Again, you cannot search and find something if you do not know to look for it!

You can use similar search techniques on most of the websites listed in this section. The object of the game is to save time and simplify where possible, AND find some great Public Domain books! Have fun. Oh, and by the way, pay attention to the book titles that are revealed during your searches. They are a great source for relevant key-words related to your niche market.

Abebooks

http://www.abebooks.com

Abebooks™ is the world's largest online marketplace for books. They makes it simple and safe to find and buy—or list and sell—new, used, rare, and out-of-print books online, with a variety of over 70 million books offered by more than 13,000 booksellers.

Comments / Notes: _____

_____

_____

Alilbris

http://www.alibris.com

Alibris connects people who love books, music and movies to thousands of independent sellers around the world. Our proprietary technology and advanced logistics allow us to offer over 50 million used, new and out-of-print books to consumers, libraries and retailers.

Comments / Notes: _____

_____

_____

Biblio Rare Book Room

http://biblio.com/rare_books.php

Biblio, the preferred online marketplace for buying and selling used, rare, and out-of-print books. We take pride in bringing together over 4000 professional, independent booksellers from around the world, to offer you over 30 million high quality used books to choose from.

Comments / Notes: _____

_____

_____

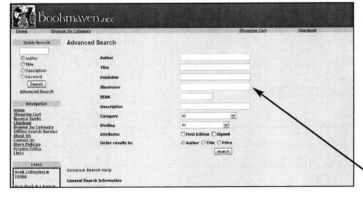

Bookmaven

http://www.bookmaven.net/

Search or browse their inventory of Antiquarian, Vintage, Out of Print, Rare & First Edition books. Most of our stock is 19th or early 20th Century and will attempt locate books they do not carry.

The Advanced Search has a unique feature that allows you to search for books by illustrator.

Comments / Notes: _____

_____

_____

Bookseller World

http://www.booksellerworld.com/

This site aims to be a complete one-stop resource site for all your book needs. Bibliographies, articles, collectors guides, book dealers and shops + much more.

The Bibliography section on this website is an awesome feature that you do not want to overlook.

Comments / Notes: _____

_____

_____

Ebay (Antiquarian / Collectible)

http://books.ebay.com/

You should be familiar with eBay Books & Magazines, and pay particular interest to the antiquarian and collectible books sections. eBay is also a fantastic source for just about any other form of Public Domain media as well as a place for selling your products.

Comments / Notes: _____

_____

_____

Powell's Books: Rare & Collectible

http://www.powells.com/rareandcollectible.html

Once you find those Public Domain treasures, this is one of the online places to go purchase them.

Comments / Notes: _____

_____

_____

Quigley's Rare Books

http://www.quigleysbooks.com/categories.html

Another source for purchasing select books in the Public Domain.

Comments / Notes: _____

_____

_____

Write in your new Public Domain Bookseller link discoveries here:

Write in your new Public Domain Bookseller link discoveries here:

_____

_____

_____

_____

_____

_____

_____

_____

_____

_____

_____

_____

_____

_____

_____

_____

_____

_____

_____

_____

_____

_____

_____

_____

_____

_____

_____

_____

_____

EPHEMERA LINKS

Ephemera refers to written and printed matter published with a short intended life-time. In the world of collectors, common types of ephemera include letters, advertising trade cards, cigarette cards, posters, postcards, baseball cards, tickets, greeting cards, stock certificates and photographs. Decks of the Most-wanted Iraqis playing cards are recent example of ephemera because they will probably lose their original purpose and interest in a relatively short time.

I've seen some creative uses of Public Domain ephemera developed into new products such as reproductions of original tobacco cards and postcards, reproduction broadsides (you've all seen the "Wanted: Dead or Alive" posters, right?), Greeting cards made from classic old pictures (some of these are brilliant), scrapbooking papers from classic ephemera and much more. Use your imagination. I've included a couple links below to get you started.

Emergence of Advertising in America Collection
http://scriptorium.lib.duke.edu/eaa/browse.html
The items included in *Emergence of Advertising in America: 1850 - 1920* (EAA) are from eleven categories. Representative samples dating from the mid 1800s to the 1920s were chosen from various collections.

Comments / Notes: _____
_____
_____

US Historical Documents
http://www.law.ou.edu/hist/
This site features a collection of United States historical documents, from the "Declaration of Independence" to a variety of speeches from our Presidents.

Comments / Notes: _____
_____
_____

Write in your new Public Domain Ephemera link discoveries here:

_____

_____

_____

_____

_____

_____

_____

_____

_____

_____

_____

_____

_____

_____

_____

_____

_____

_____

_____

_____

_____

_____

_____

_____

_____

_____

_____

ART / PHOTOGRAPHY LINKS

✦

I am thrilled to include this section on art and photography because it reflects a large part of who I am, being a graphic artist by trade and having worked as a commercial photographer as well. I LOVE art in all its forms. And because of my passion in this media area, I have located some really excellent resources for you to discover for yourself just how beautiful the world of the Public Domain can be.

If you spent any time searching through the Publisher Links section, you will have seen some fantastic uses of classic art and photography, from collections to reproductions and all points inbetween. I do want to caution you however not to allow those sites to limit your creativity. Very often, we will see art or photography used in a certain way that appeals to us, so we set out to do our OWN version of what someone else has done. That's okay, and you may be successful with it, but why not move beyond what others have done to create new and exciting possibilities? The only thing stopping you is YOU.

A note about formats: As you begin to discover images you want to save and use, you will notice that they will be usually be available in one of a variety of file formats. The most common formats used are JPEG, GIF, TIFF, PNG, JPEG2000 and MrSID. To successfully work with some of these formats, you will want to have image processing software such as Photoshop or Photoshop Elements. You can easily open and manipulate the JPEG, GIF, TIFF and PNG file formats right out of the box. To view JPEG2000 and MrSID (you'll find files using these compression schemes on the Library of Congress website and others) in your web browser, you will want to download the freely available plug-in available from LizardTech called ExpressView Browser Plug-in. You can download it at the LizardTech website (http://www.lizardtech.com/download/index.php).

There is also a standalone MrSID browser available for download at the Library of Congress website (http://memory.loc.gov/ammem/help/download_sid.html). I would highly recommend using this browser for MrSID images because it has a feature that allows you to export the images at full resolution as TIFF images...a very important feature if you want to take advantage of those high resolution scans available on the LOC website.

A free JPEG2000 plugin for Photoshop and Paintshop Pro is also available from Lead Technologies. You can download the plug-in from the Lead Technologies website at: http://www.leadtools.com/utilities/psplugin/PhotoShop_plug-in.htm. This is extremely handy to have if you use Photoshop or Paintshop Pro since it enables you to open and save files with the JPEG2000 file format. In other words...go download it.

Money-saving tip

As I mentioned earlier, to work with images you will need an image-processing program like Adobe Photoshop Elements. And if you want to take some of those images and stylize them as digital paintings using digital natural media tools, you will need a software package like Corel Painter Essentials. These programs each sell for around $85-$90...and that's a pretty good deal. But here is a better deal: The Wacom Graphire4 4x5 USB Tablet features a cordless pressure sensitive pen AND a cordless mouse. It is totally amazing and sells for less than $90. What sweetens the deal even more is the bundled software. You've guessed it...it comes with copies of both Photoshop Elements AND Painter Essentials, along a number of other excellent programs as well. For the cost of just one of the programs, you can actually pick up both and the tablet for the same price. This is really a no brainer purchase! Get you own tablet at The Graphics Expert (www.thegraphicsexpert.com). And while you are there, make sure you check out their excellent selection of tools needed for working with all types of Public Domain media.

American Museum of Natural History

http://digitallibrary.amnh.org/dspace/

AMNH scientific publications disseminate the results of laboratory investigations and fieldwork conducted by museum scientists and their colleagues in the areas of zoological systematics, paleontology, geology, evolution, and anthropology.

Comments / Notes: _____

_____

_____

_____

David Rumsey Collection

http://www.davidrumsey.com/

The David Rumsey Historical Map Collection has over 12,600 maps online. The collection focuses on rare 18th and 19th century North and South America maps and other cartographic materials. Historic maps of the World, Europe, Asia and Africa are also represented.

Comments / Notes: _____

_____

_____

_____

Department of Agriculture Image Gallery

http://www.ars.usda.gov/is/graphics/photos/index.html

The Image Gallery is provided as a complimentary source of high quality digital photographs available from the Agricultural Research Service Information Staff. Select a category from the left to view images with caption information, or in a proof sheet format without captions.

Comments / Notes: _____

_____

_____

_____

Department of the Interior Photo Resources Library

http://www.doi.gov/gallery.html

The Photo Library for the Department of the Interior. Also includes links to other relevant government websites that contain images.

Check out the other websites listed here as well for even more images.

Comments / Notes: _____

_____

_____

_____

Great Images in NASA (GRIN)

http://grin.hq.nasa.gov/

GRIN is a collection of over a thousand images of significant historical interest scanned at high-resolution in several sizes. This collection is intended for the media, publishers, and the general public looking for high-quality photographs.

Comments / Notes: _____

_____

_____

_____

Hortus Nitidissimis

http://www.kew.org/hortus/default.jsp

A year in a brilliant garden of exquisite flowers represented in beautiful pictures. This a classic horticulture book available online.

For more images, be sure to explore the collections area.

Comments / Notes: _____

_____

_____

_____

Images of American Political History

http://teachpol.tcnj.edu/amer_pol_hist/

All images in this collection of American Political History photographs are strongly believed to be in the public domain. They were obtained from non-copyrighted U.S. government holdings and publications and from published works with clearly expired copyrights.

Comments / Notes: _____

_____

_____

_____

Images in the Public Domain

http://srufaculty.sru.edu/david.dailey/public/public_domain.htm

This is a collection of illustrations from a variety of subjects that were scanned from an early Webster's Dictionary.

Comments / Notes: _____

_____

_____

_____

Morgue File

http://www.morguefile.com/archive/

This site provides the public and creative community with free raw photo materials. Don't let the name fool you. There are a lot of great images here. They are NOT in the Public Domain but ARE still free to use privately and commercially.

Comments / Notes: _____

_____

_____

_____

National Park Service Digital Image Archive

http://photo.itc.nps.gov/storage/images/index.html

This site provides links to public domain digital images of many of those sites, including national parks, monuments, historic sites and related areas in both JPG and Photo CD formats.

Comments / Notes: _____

_____

_____

_____

New York Public Library Digital Gallery

http://digitalgallery.nypl.org

NYPL Digital Gallery provides access to over 415,000 images digitized from primary sources and printed rarities in the collections of The New York Public Library.

Comments / Notes: _____

_____

_____

_____

NOAA Historical Maps and Charts

http://nauticalcharts.noaa.gov/csdl/ctp/

The Office of Coast Survey's Historical Map & Chart Collection contains over 20,000 maps and charts from the late 1700s to present day.

You can find the historic maps here, but there are also many other gems to be mined on this site as well.

Comments / Notes: _____

_____

_____

_____

_____

NOAA Photo Library

http://www.photolib.noaa.gov/collections.html

The NOAA Photo Library has been produced to help bring the work of one of America's most remarkable Government agencies to the American people.

Comments / Notes: _____
_____
_____
_____

Online Archive of California

http://findaid.oac.cdlib.org/search.image.html

We provide access to tens of thousands of photographs, paintings, graphical materials and other types of images.

Comments / Notes: _____
_____
_____
_____

Public Domain Photo Database

http://pdphoto.org/

PDPhoto.org is a repository for free public domain photos. Unless something is clearly marked as being copyrighted, you can assume it is free to use.

The links page will net you even more photos in the Public Domain.

Comments / Notes: _____
_____
_____
_____

PhotoGraphic Libraries

http://www.photographiclibraries.com/index.php

The stock images, film and photo archives listed provide a creative source for television producers, advertising agencies, libraries, education centers, picture researchers and Photojournalist researching visual communications—contains national and private photographic collections.

Comments / Notes: _____
_____
_____
_____

Pictures Catalogue

http://www.nla.gov.au/apps/picturescatalogue

This catalogue contains descriptions of paintings, drawings, prints, photographs and three-dimensional objects held in the Pictures Collection of the National Library of Australia. The Pictures Collection contains approximately 45,000 paintings and over 600,000 photographs; most of this material has been catalogued with individual descriptions or collection summaries.

Comments / Notes: _____

_____

_____

_____

Prints With a Past

http://www.printspast.com/index.htm

Prints with a Past provides original antique prints, engravings and lithographs on topics including botanicals, natural history prints, children's prints, sports, landscapes, maps, fashions and much more! If you're looking for Public Domain original prints to reproduce, this is the place to shop.

Comments / Notes: _____

_____

_____

_____

Shigitatsu

http://www.shigitatsu.com/

Rare antique illustrated botanical and natural history books, original antique botanical and natural history prints, Digital art and fine art reproductions.

Comments / Notes: _____

_____

_____

_____

US Fish and Wildlife Services Images

http://www.fws.gov/pictures/

The U.S. Fish and Wildlife Service's online digital media library. Presently, the library system contains the National Image Library—the Service's collection of public domain still photos.

Follow the deer to even MORE fish and wildlife images in the Public Domain.

Comments / Notes: _____

_____

_____

US Government Graphics and Photos

http://www.firstgov.gov/Topics/Graphics.shtml

This is a treasure trove listing of government websites that have image links. Most of the images are in the Public Domain.

Comments / Notes: _____

_____

_____

_____

Ward Maps

http://www.wardmaps.com/index.htm

Ward Maps is your online source for authentic antique and archival prints of urban maps.

They specialize in the digital restoration and archival printing of neighborhood maps of American cities.

Comments / Notes: _____

_____

_____

_____

Wikipedia Free Images

http://en.wikipedia.org/wiki/Wikipedia: List_of_images

The purpose of this page is to provide a browsable repository of images that are available on Wikipedia. Only public domain, copyleft, and otherwise free images are included in this repository.

Even more Public Domain media in the Commons.

Comments / Notes: _____

_____

_____

_____

Wikimedia Commons Public Domain Collection

http://commons.wikimedia.org/wiki/Category:Public_domain

An Amazing collections of all types of Public Domain materials and resources, from audio and art work to books and videos.

Comments / Notes: _____

_____

_____

_____

Yellowstone National Park Images

http://www.nps.gov/yell/press/images/

Yellowstone National Park has created this page to provide over 9,000 publication-quality images for use by the media and the general public. These images are in the public domain and are available for use, free of charge.

Comments / Notes: _____

_____

_____

Yoto Photo

http://yotophoto.com/

Yotophoto is the first internet search engine for finding free-to-use stock photographs and images. Now indexing over 150,000 Creative Commons, Public Domain, GNU FDL, and various other 'copyleft' images.

Comments / Notes: _____

_____

_____

Write in your new Public Domain Art / Photography link discoveries here:

_____

_____

_____

_____

_____

_____

_____

_____

_____

_____

_____

_____

_____

_____

_____

_____

_____

_____

_____

_____

_____

_____

_____

_____

_____

_____

AUDIO / VIDEO LINKS

※

Remember that classic Bugs Bunny cartoon where he goes head-to-head with the airplane gremlin? I love that cartoon...Bugs Bunny rocks! Did you know that cartoon and many others are in the Public Domain? It IS and you can download it right now, burn it onto a DVD and sell it, along with Sherlock Holmes movies, and a huge number of other classics. But classics are not the only types of video or audio files that await you in the Public Domain. Much of the video footage shot by our government and government agencies is also in the Public Domain, along with audio recordings of speeches, interviews, congressional hearings, etc. It's all out there waiting for you.

Perhaps you are thinking, "Who would buy DVD's or CD's of Public Domain media?" You have a point. I mean, after all, I am sure by now you have been to a Dollar store and have seen DVD's for a buck. Or maybe you saw cheap DVD's in the check-out line at Walmart. So if Walmart is selling them for a buck, then they can't be worth much right? Trust me...you are asking the wrong question. The question to ask is this: "Why is Walmart even bothering in the first place?" There's a good reason for it and the answer is simple...because they sell. Look around on Ebay or check out some of the Publisher Links listed earlier in the book. You will see some inventive uses for Public Domain audio and video media. Check out some of the vendors who sell the stuff on Ebay...like classic video collections. Track their sales. You will see what I am talking about.

My challenge to you again is to use your imagination. There are many terrific resources out there waiting to be discovered. Find them and create something people will want. Use them as bonuses, or to boost back-end sales. Create a site where people can view streaming versions of the shows. Pull together collections of thematic documentaries, or use excerpts along with original video. The possibilities are endless.

Let me even challenge you with one more possibility: iPod® Video. There are a number of sites included in this book where you can grab hundreds of movies and documentaries. You can convert them to play on Video iPods® then sell them to that market (which is growing quickly, BTW). Again, the possiblities are endless.

Now there are a few tools of the trade that you will want to consider adding to your arsenal if you plan to work with audio or video media. I suggest you take a look at some of Sony's excellent products (http://www.sonymediasoftware.com/) such as Sound Forge Audio Studio 8 for working with sound files, or Vegas Movie Studio+DVD 6 for working with the video files. You can learn more about these excellent tools on the Sony Media Software website. Plus, they will cost you less than a hundred bucks each. I have been using the pro versions of this software for years and can attest to how easy they are to use. I guarantee you will be having fun with new creations in no time.

BuyOut Footage

http://www.buyoutfootage.com/

Buyout Footage is a full service stock footage house featuring the very best in contemporary royalty free stock footage, full-length public domain films and archive film stock footage.

Comments / Notes: _____
_____
_____
_____

Desert Island Films, Inc.

http://www.desertislandfilms.com/

Public Domain films, Public Domain movies, and Public Domain videos, all high broadcast quality, are available from Desert Island Films, Inc., the largest and oldest source for public domain films and TV programs in the world.

Comments / Notes: _____
_____
_____
_____

Digiview Productions

http://www.digiviewus.com/pages/productshome.html

Digiview Productions was established in January of 2004, launching itself into the value priced DVD sales world. Our mission is to lead the distribution of DVD's to the retail market with favorite screen writes and animations from assorted genres.

Comments / Notes: _____
_____
_____

Festival Films

http://www.fesfilms.com/

Festival Films has been in business for over 30 years selling 16mm Films, Videotapes, Movie Posters and now DVDs and has the largest public domain collection in the world. Best quality from 1" Masters.

Scroll down to "Video Masters" then to "Gallery of Movie Posters of Public Domain Films!" for a cool surprise.

Comments / Notes: _____
_____
_____
_____

Film Chest

http://filmchest.com/

Film Chest's programming is professionally transferred from library masters in both PAL and NTSC formats. Our public domain content may be utilized for broadcast, duplication or resale without restriction

Comments / Notes: _____

_____

_____

_____

Jim's Rare Serials & B-Westerns

http://www.rareserials.com/

Jim has been building his collection of the best rare serials, movies and television shows for over 20 years. He deals with other collectors all over the world to ensure that his videos are of the best quality available anywhere.

Comments / Notes: _____

_____

_____

_____

LibriVox

http://librivox.org/

LibriVox volunteers record chapters of books in the public domain, and we release the audio files back into the public domain.

LibriVox provides some wonderful information in their wiki help section...be sure to read through it.

Comments / Notes: _____

_____

_____

_____

Like Television...Only Better

http://tesla.liketelevision.com/

LikeTelevision - The Broadband Media Network, is a recognized leader in delivering video applications over public (Internet) and private networks. In 1999, the company developed the IGS process, which creates high quality video files at very low data rates.

Comments / Notes: _____

_____

_____

_____

OpenFlix

http://www.openflix.com/

OpenFlix provides a directory of movies commonly thought to be in the public domain, related resources, and a discussion forum. In addition, OpenFlix works with copyright holders who wish to gain widespread distribution of their works through the Internet.

Comments / Notes: _____

_____

_____

_____

Pan American Video

http://www.panamvideo.com/index.html

PAN AMERICAN VIDEO has zillions of public domain stock footage clips pulled from our vast library of broadcast quality masters. Our archives are chocked full of vintage feature films, TV shows, cartoons, documentaries, movie trailers and other stuff that act as sources for your clips.

Comments / Notes: _____

_____

_____

_____

The Public Domain Movie Database

http://pdmdb.org/

An In-Depth, Detailed Look at your Favorite Public-Domain Movies. A Searchable Database of Public-Domain Movie Information, Episode Guides and More.

Comments / Notes: _____

_____

_____

_____

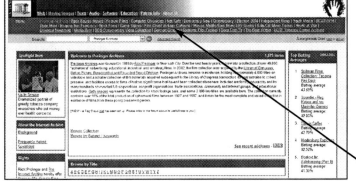

Prelinger Archives

http://www.archive.org/details/prelinger

Prelinger Archives remains in existence, holding approximately 4,000 titles on videotape and a smaller collection of film materials acquired subsequent to the Library of Congress transaction.

Have fun digging around on this excellent, and while you're at it, be sure to visit one of my favorite sections, Film Chest Vintage Cartoons.

Comments / Notes: _____

_____

_____

_____

Public Domain Torrents

http://www.publicdomaintorrents.com/

Downloads hundreds of Public Domain movies to play of the digital device of your choice.

Comments / Notes: _____

_____

_____

Radio Lovers

http://www.radiolovers.com/

We offer hundreds of vintage radio shows for you to listen to online in mp3 format, all for free.

Skip right to the complete list to find Abbott and Costello, Superman, Groucho Marx, The Avenger, Gunsmoke, Sherlock Homes, and many others.

Comments / Notes: _____

_____

_____

_____

RetroFilm Media

http://www.retrofilm.com/

RetroFilm Media International specializes in providing media professionals with high broadcast quality programming content for use in broadcast television, film projects, video streaming, distribution, public television, cable or other professional needs.

Comments / Notes: _____

_____

_____

_____

Shokus Video

http://www.shokus.com/

Shokus Video has been a leader in supplying classic 1950s TV shows to the home video market since 1979! Now you can relive the golden days of live television all over again with our large library of classic programming on both DVD and VHS!

Comments / Notes: _____

_____

_____

_____

TV Video

http://www.tvideo.com/index.htm

TV Video offers classic programs in many categories including: animated, comedy, crime, documentary, drama, sci-fi, war, western and others.

Comments / Notes: _____

_____

_____

The Video Beat

http://www.thevideobeat.com/store/index.php

The VIDEO BEAT! is your source for rare 1950s & 1960s rock n roll movies and TV shows. If you're searching for movies featuring rock n roll, juvenile delinquents, hippies, hot rods, clean teens or beatnik anti-establishment types, then you're in luck! We've got 'em all on DVD and VHS!

Comments / Notes: _____

_____

_____

Write in your new Public Domain Audio / Video link discoveries here:

_____

_____

_____

_____

_____

_____

_____

_____

_____

_____

_____

_____

_____

_____

_____

_____

_____

_____

_____

_____

_____

_____

_____

_____

_____

- 76 - www.publicdomaincodebook.com

LINK COLLECTION LINKS

I could have gone through the links pages in this section and just listed every webpage that featured Public Domain media, but why rob you of the joy of the hunt, not to mention it would have taken me a very long time...yikes! The fact is, there are thousands of links to pour over and dig through on the following pages. Some are thematically related, others are not. Also note that not ALL the links you find will lead you to Public Domain materials. Make sure you read copyright notices and terms of use statements.

These types of pages are for those of you who love to sort through pages of links like the example you see at left. (you are working through this books so you must like it some). Rabbit trails can be fun but also time consuming. I like to think of it more as panning for gold. So go dig out your digital pan and hit the streams of data to pan for gold. Depending on what you are looking for, you might just strike it rich.

Digital Collections Online (University of Connecticut)

http://webapps.lib.uconn.edu/DigitalCollections/default.cfm

Digital Collections Online (DCO) is a resource that includes information about and links to digital collections worldwide, which range in subject from classic American sheet music and Connecticut history to Victorian literature.

Comments / Notes: _____

_____

_____

_____

Digital Librarian (Electronic Texts)

http://www.digital-librarian.com/electronic.html

Margaret Vail Anderson, a librarian in Cortland, New York, has collected hundreds of her favorite resources. Known as a librarian's choice of the best of the Web, the Digital Librarian is an amazing treasure trove of places to locate Public Domain resources.

Comments / Notes: _____

_____

_____

_____

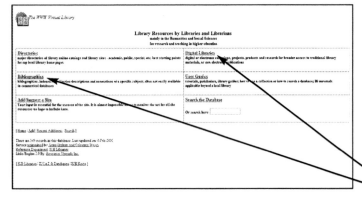

Library Resources by Libraries and Librarians

http://www.indiana.edu/~vlib/

The title speaks for itself. This is another research Mecca for finding old books.

Start your search in "Digital Libraries," but also search the "Bibliography" section as well.

Comments / Notes: _____

_____

_____

_____

Links to New Thought Texts

http://religiousscience.us/links/texts_nt.htm

This site contains comprehensive directories of New Thought & Spiritual Texts.

Comments / Notes: _____

_____

_____

_____

Online Books Page

http://onlinebooks.library.upenn.edu/

The Online Books Page is a website that facilitates access to books that are freely readable over the Internet. It currently provides access to over 25,000 books.

Comments / Notes: _____
_____
_____
_____

Southwest Electronic Text Library

http://dizzy.library.arizona.edu/swetc/other.html

A collection of links to e-text centers from around the web.

Comments / Notes: _____
_____
_____
_____

Voice of the Shuttle

http://vos.ucsb.edu/

The Voice of the Shuttle provides over 70 pages of links to humanities and humanities-related resources on the Internet.

Comments / Notes: _____
_____
_____
_____

WESS Web: Electronic Texts Collection

http://www.lib.virginia.edu/wess/etexts.html

This page lists Internet sources for literary texts in the western European languages other than English.

This link will take you to more listings of links arranged by country.

Comments / Notes: _____
_____
_____
_____

Women's Studies Database Reading Room

http://www.mith2.umd.edu/WomensStudies/ReadingRoom/History/

A nice collection of historical links pertaining to women's studies and issues.

Comments / Notes: _____

_____

_____

_____

Write in your new Link Collection link discoveries here:

_____

_____

_____

_____

_____

_____

_____

_____

_____

_____

_____

_____

_____

_____

_____

_____

_____

_____

_____

_____

_____

_____

_____

_____

_____

_____

_____

_____

Write in your new Link Collection link discoveries here:

_____

_____

_____

_____

_____

_____

_____

_____

_____

_____

_____

_____

_____

_____

_____

_____

_____

_____

_____

_____

_____

_____

_____

_____

_____

BOOK SEARCH LINKS

—⋙⋘—

The Internet rises and falls with the use of search engines, especially since their job is to help you find what you are looking for. Obviously, they will also be of great use to you in finding Public Domain materials. While I'm sure you are familiar with the top search engines like Google, Yahoo and MSN, the search websites I have included in this section are not your typical search engines. They are specifically designed to help you search for books...except for one. I decided to also include Answers.com in this section because of the amazing amount of information you can find there related to Public Domain books. However, there is a trick to finding the treasure (isn't there always?). You are in luck though because I discovered that trick (by accident actually) and am going to spill the beans. How would you like step-by-step instructions on how to use Answers.com to discover some amazing Public Domain works? I figured you would say yes. Here you go...

Okay...first things first...you COULD go to the website's main page and begin to search there for Public Domain books. It IS a search portal after all, but you will have a much harder time locating the books you are looking for. I don't know about you, but I like to find things the EASY way. So that being said, launch your web browser and type in the the website's address. But instead of just typing in the main site, use the following address:  www.answers.com/topic/<YEAR>, where <YEAR> is the publishing year for the books we want to find (in other words, do not type in "<YEAR>." You want to type an actual year, like 1902 in the place of "<YEAR>". Now remember, all books published in the year 1922 or earlier are now in the Public Domain, as well as approximately 80% of the books published between the years of 1923 and 1964. For now, we'll keep it simple and stick with books that we know for sure are in the Public Domain. Using my earlier example of 1902, complete the web address so that it looks like this: www.answers.com/topic/1902. Once you have typed in the address, hit <ENTER>.

 www.publicdomaincodebook.com

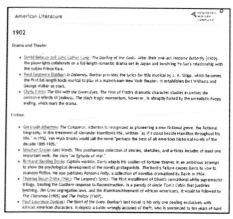

The first thing you will notice on the resulting page is a section on Science and Technology. This is NOT what we are looking for. What WE are looking for is the "American Literature" section. Scroll down the page until you come to the American Literature section, or use the drop-down navigation menu located at the top of the screen and select "US Literature." When you get to the American Literature section, you will see a number of sub-categories listed including Drama and Theater, Fiction, Nonfiction, Poetry and Publications and Events.

Now here is an exciting nugget of treasure...all the authors and books you see listed in these sections are ALL in the Public Domain! Now before you go off on the rabbit trails (there will be time for that later), let's dig a little deeper.

Scroll down through the sections until you come to the Nonfiction section. Locate an author named Charles Eastman (he is my favorite Native American author). The entry will look like this:

Charles Eastman (1858-1939): *Indian Boyhood.* One of the earliest Native American autobiographies captures Eastman's first fifteen years as a traditional hunter and warrior in Minnesota and Canada. The work makes Eastman the most widely known Native American writer in the first decades of the twentieth century. It would be followed by three collections of short stories dealing with Sioux traditions and history—*Red Hunters and the Animal People* (1904), *Old Indian Days* (1907), and *Wigwam Days* (1909)—and a continuation of his autobiography, *From the Deep Woods to Civilization* (1916).

Click on the author's name. You will notice that the resulting page contains a listing of books by the author, an author biography, links to online works by the author, and much, much more. It doesn't get any easier than this, folks!

Okay...hit the "Back" button...let's look at another author. Scroll up a bit until you are in the "Fiction" section. Click on "Jack London," another of my favorite authors. Again you'll see a massive amount of info about the author that includes a complete bibliography and links to many of his books available online. Yes, this is THAT easy! I TOLD you!

Now, here is another secret for this website: go back up to the web address line and type in another year and hit <ENTER>. Pick a year, **any** year. Follow the same instructions and see what you discover. That's it...amazing isn't it?

What is so wonderful about this website is that Answers.com takes a lot of the guesswork out of identifying outstanding books and authors that are now in the Public Domain. This is valuable information that I encourage you to explore. You never know what gem you just might uncover!

Have fun with it! Oh...and make sure you check out the other search sites in this section as well.

UPDATE ON GOOGLE'S BOOK SEARCH

Download the Classics: 8/30/2006

Posted by Adam Mathes, Associate Product Manager, Google Book Search

Starting today, you can go to Google Book Search and download full copies of out-of-copyright books to read at your own pace. You're free to choose from a diverse collection of public domain titles—from well-known classics to obscure gems.

Before the rise of the public library—a story chronicled in this 1897 edition of The Free Library—access to large collections of books was the privilege of a wealthy minority. Now, with the help of our wonderful library partners, we're able to offer you the ability to download and read PDF versions of out-of-copyright books from some of the world's greatest collections.

Using Google Book Search, you can find The Free Library and many other extraordinary old books, such as:

- Ferriar's The Bibliomania
- A futurist from 1881's 1931: A Glance at the Twentieth Century
- Aesop's Fables
- Shakespeare's Hamlet
- Abbott's Flatland
- Hugo's Marion De Lorme
- Dunant's Eine Erinnerung an Solferino
- Bolívar's Proclamas
- Dante's Inferno

Continued on page 87

AddALL Used and Out of Print Search

http://used.addall.com/

AddALL is a free service that searches for the best deal in books anywhere on-line. It was built by book buyers for book buyers. AddALL is an independent and impartial web site, not owned by any bookstore. The search result is therefore totally objective.

Comments / Notes: _____

_____

_____

Answers.com

http://www.answers.com

This is a website of answers...and certainly does not disappoint when it comes to finding Public Domain books, if you know where to look. Make sure you read the introduction to this section for some great tips to locating books.

Comments / Notes: _____

_____

_____

Bibliofind

http://www.bibliofind.com

Bibliofind has combined with Amazon.com to provide millions of rare, used, and out-of-print books through the world's No.1 online bookstore. Search for millions of hard-to-find titles from their trusted community of Bibliofind and Amazon.com booksellers.

Comments / Notes: _____

_____

_____

Book Sales Finder

http://www.book-sales-in-america.com/

Here you'll find thousands of book sales, book fairs, book auctions, and other book events held throughout the USA and Canada. Just click on a state to get a calendar of events.

Scroll down the page to the United States map. Click on the state of your choice to find a listing of every upcoming book show, book sale and library sale.

Comments / Notes: _____

_____

_____

_____

BookFinder

http://www.bookfinder.com

BookFinder.com is the open marketplace for books online—a one stop ecommerce search engine where you can search through over 100 million new, used, rare, and out of print books for sale.

Comments / Notes: _____
_____
_____

Google Book Search

http://www.books.google.com/

Google Print is making available a number of public domain books that were never subject to copyright or whose copyright has expired. Search the full text of books to find ones that interest you.

You will want to "View Full Books." Also Google's Advanced Search allows you to enter publishing years...very important.

Comments / Notes: _____
_____
_____
_____

Used Books Search

http://www.used-books-search.com

A used books meta search engine for second hand, rare, out of print books and text books. Search, browse and buy online from thousands of bookstores worldwide.

Comments / Notes: _____
_____
_____

Continued from page 85

To find out-of-copyright books that you can download, simply select the "Full view" radio button when you search on books.google.com. (Please note that we do not enable downloading of any book currently under copyright. Unless we have the publisher's permission to show more, we display only small snippets of text—at most, two or three sentences surrounding your search term—to help you determine if you've found what you're looking for.)

Of course, this is just the beginning. As we digitize more of the world's books—whether rare, common, popular or obscure—people everywhere will be able to discover them on Google Book Search.

www.publicdomaincodebook.com

Write in your new Public Domain Book Search link discoveries here:

_____

_____

_____

_____

_____

_____

_____

_____

_____

_____

_____

_____

_____

_____

_____

_____

_____

_____

_____

_____

_____

_____

_____

_____

_____

_____

_____

_____

GOVERNMENT LINKS

✦✦✦

The United States government is the single largest publisher in the world. Every year, millions of documents are published by the Federal government, from transcripts of speeches to how-to manuals to legal records. These government documents can be of tremendous value to journalists and other information gatherers, because they provide access to more detailed information on more subjects than any other source. Although some US documents are classified as "top secret," the vast majority are available to the public and are in the Public Domain. The FirstGov website alone features a database of over 30 million documents, and that represents just one government source of many. Please note that not ALL government items are in the Public Domain, but most are. Make sure you read copyright notices where available.

Locating media that may be of interest to you is in many case as straight forward as using a search engine with keywords. What you may discover, however, is that the report you want will cost you, which, in the grand scheme of things, may not be a big deal. It would be no different than purchasing a Public Domain book at a used bookstore or online. What I have discovered though is that with some creative searching, you can often find the document you want for free. Free is better. Let me give you an example.

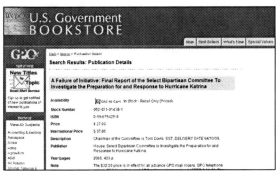

The U.S. Government recently released reports concerning the governmental response to the Katrina disaster. Both the Office of the President and the Select Bipartisan Committee released separate reports. Let's say you want to locate the report produced by the Select Bipartisan Committee. It is titled, "Failure of Initiative." You could go to the Government Bookstore website (http://bookstore.gpo.gov/), do a keyword search for "Katrina" or for the title itself. Click on the link that the search provides and you can pick up a perfect-bound copy of this excellent report for $27. Pretty easy.

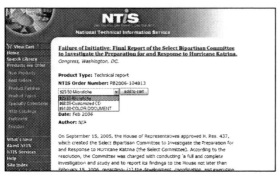

Another option for you would be to go to the The National Technical Information Service (NTIS), at www.ntis.gov, perform a search again for "Katrina" and select the search result that pertains to "Failure of Initiative." Here you will find the report available on microfiche, customized CD or as a color document. You will also notice that the associated cost for this report is even higher on this website ($29.50, $68.00 and $91.00 respectively).

The final option is to get the report for free...the choice is yours. I like free. Here's how you do it. You know that the report is titled "Failure of Initiative." Go to the FirstGov website (www.firstgov.gov) and perform a search for the report title making sure you enclose the title in parentheses. What you will discover first on the search results list is a link to the website for the Select Bipartisan Committee (katrina.house.gov). Click on the link and you will discover something amazing. The entire report is listed in PDF form and available for free download. Free IS better!

This little trick will work for many of the Government documents that are available. Of course you could just go to FirstGov from the beginning, but the advantage to digging around at the Government Bookstore and NTIS (as well as other government websites) is that they often identify the most searched for or most popular documents. This is valuable to know since you do not want something that people are not interested in. In any event, you will find a massive amount of fantastic information available on these sites. I don't want to give up all the secret treasure awaiting you, but here are a few examples...all the NASA space footage, census information, training manuals, health and fitness manuals and guidelines, National Park Service photographs, and much more await your discovery.

Also note that this is not an all-inclusive set of links for Government sites. I left many out so that you could enjoy hunting for some of that Government Gold for yourself. Just bear this in mind...EVERY section of the government has their own website and resources, making this one of the largest treasure fields you will ever explore. It's almost like having your very own personal Fort Knox...without all the red tape and security.

19th Century in Print

http://memory.loc.gov/ammem/ndlpcoop/moahtml/mnchome.html

The books in this collection bear nineteenth century American imprints, dating mainly from between 1850 and 1880. They have been digitized by the University of Michigan as part of the *Making of America* project, a major collaborative endeavor to preserve and provide access to historical texts. Currently, approximately 1,500 books are included. The collection is particularly strong in poetry and in the subject areas of education, psychology, American history, sociology, religion, and science and technology.

Comments / Notes: _____
_____
_____
_____

Academic Info (US Government Publications)

http://www.academicinfo.net/gdocsus.html

Comments / Notes: _____
_____
_____
_____

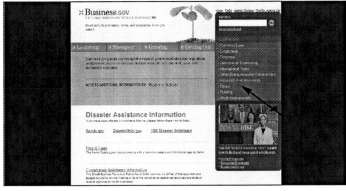

Business.gov

http://www.business.gov/

Business.gov guides you through the maze of government rules and regulations and provides access to services and resources to help you start, grow, and succeed in business.

There are many useful tools here including this section on Resource and Research.

Comments / Notes: _____
_____
_____
_____

Google Search for Government Resources

http://www.google.com/unclesam

Comments / Notes: _____
_____
_____
_____

Government Accountability Office

http://www.gao.gov/index.html
The Official Web Site of the Government Accountability Office.

Comments / Notes: _____
_____
_____
_____

Government Document Brochures and Pamphlets

http://libweb.lib.buffalo.edu/cts/GovDocBP/
This digital collection contains selected general interest publications produced by the U.S. Federal Government and received by the University at Buffalo Libraries through the Federal Depository Library Program.

Comments / Notes: _____
_____
_____
_____

Government Reports

http://www.govspot.com/news/reports/
GovSpot.com is a non-partisan government information portal designed to simplify the search for the best and most relevant government information online. This free resource offers a high-utility collection of top government and civic resources hand-selected by their editorial team for their quality, content and utility.

Comments / Notes: _____
_____
_____
_____

Government Reports on Environment

http://www.lib.washington.edu/subject/environment/gov.html
The University of Washington Libraries collection of Government reports on the environment.

Find additional resources here from both governmental and non-governmental sources.

Comments / Notes: _____
_____
_____

Indiana University Government Database

http://www.ulib.iupui.edu/subjectareas/gov/dbsubject.html

Comments / Notes: _____

_____

_____

Library of Congress

http://www.loc.gov/index.html

I think this site is pretty self-explanatory. You can literally spend days going through all the offerings on this site and not exhaust them. Look here for images, movies, books, art, etc.

Global Gateway is a wonderful source for Multilingual resources on world culture and just one of many treasures waiting to be looted on this amazing site.

Comments / Notes: _____

_____

_____

_____

The National Archives

http://www.archives.gov/

Of all documents and materials created in the course of business conducted by the United States Federal government, only 1%-3% are so important for legal or historical reasons that they are kept by us forever. Those valuable records are preserved and are available to you, whether you want to see if they contain clues about your family's history, need to prove a veteran's military service, or are researching an historical topic that interests you.

Comments / Notes: _____

_____

_____

_____

National Audiovisual Center

http://www.ntis.gov/products/nac

NAC is a unique centralized resource for federally developed training and education materials. Its collection contains over 9,000 audiovisual and media productions. The range of subject areas includes training in occupational safety and health, fire services, law enforcement, and foreign languages. Information and educational materials include areas such as history, health, agriculture, and natural resources.

Comments / Notes: _____

_____

_____

National Parks Service Photo Archive

http://photo.itc.nps.gov/storage/images/index.html

This site provides links to public domain digital images of many of those sites, including national parks, monuments, historic sites and related areas in both JPG and Photo CD formats.

Comments / Notes: _____

_____

_____

_____

NTIS

http://www.ntis.gov/index.asp

The National Technical Information Service provides information on more than 600,000 information products covering over 350 subject areas from over 200 federal agencies.

This is a great place to start. Here you can preview a number of videos available from the Government.

Comments / Notes: _____

_____

_____

_____

OSU Repository for Government Documents

http://www.library.okstate.edu/govdocs/

Comments / Notes: _____

_____

_____

_____

Science Gov

http://www.science.gov/

Science.gov is a gateway to authoritative selected science information provided by U.S. Government agencies, including research and development results. Enables you to search 47 million pages in real time

Comments / Notes: _____

_____

_____

_____

Technical Reports

http://www2.lib.udel.edu/subj/godc/resguide/techrpt.htm

Technical reports are written as part of government funded research on a variety of subjects. Most federal government funded research is performed by universities, nonprofit organizations and industries under contract to government agencies. This is a very comprehensive site for this type of Public Domain resource.

Comments / Notes: _____
_____
_____
_____

US Government Printing Office

http://www.gpoaccess.gov/

Kind of self-explanatory. This is a great place to find government reports on a wide variety of subjects and topics.

Comments / Notes: _____
_____
_____
_____

U.S. Government Graphics and Photos

http://www.firstgov.gov/Topics/Graphics.shtml

Most of these images and graphics are available for use in the public domain; they may be used and reproduced without permission or fee.

To find additional reference resources in addition to the graphics or photo resources on this site, go to the FirstGov Reference Center.

Comments / Notes: _____
_____
_____
_____

U.S. Government Reference Center

http://www.firstgov.gov/Topics/Reference_Shelf.shtml

Comments / Notes: _____
_____
_____
_____

Yellowstone National Park Press Images

http://www.nps.gov/yell/press/images/

Yellowstone National Park has created this page to provide over 12,000 publication-quality images for use by the media and the general public. These images are in the public domain and are available for use, free of charge.

Comments / Notes: _____

_____

_____

———————⇒•⇐———————

Write in your new Public Domain Government link discoveries here:

_____

_____

_____

_____

_____

_____

_____

_____

_____

_____

_____

_____

_____

_____

_____

_____

_____

_____

_____

_____

INFORMATION LINKS

❧❧

My quest for Public Domain websites has taken me all over the world. I have learned SO much through this process. While searching for the sites contained in this book, I came across a few excellent information resources directly related to the Public Domain. While this book is not intended to provided an in-depth study on all the aspects of the Public Domain, there are some excellent resources available both online and offline that do. The links included below will take you to a few of those resources. I would encourage you to take the time to learn from these websites. It will only serve to make your experiences in the Public Domain better ones.

───────

Google Blog: Public Domain

http://googleblog.blogspot.com/2005/11/preserving-public-domain-books.html
Google's information site on the public domain...lots of good information here!

Comments / Notes: _____
_____
_____
_____

Intellectual Properties Information Center (Kansas State University)

http://www.k-state.edu/academicservices/intprop/pub_domain_materials.htm
Great place to begin searching, not only for Public Domain resources with the links they provide, but also for info about the Public Domain.

Comments / Notes: _____
_____
_____
_____

Write in your new Public Domain Information link discoveries here:

_____

_____

_____

_____

_____

_____

_____

_____

_____

_____

_____

_____

_____

_____

_____

_____

_____

_____

_____

_____

_____

_____

_____

_____

_____

_____

_____

_____

LAST MINUTE ADDITIONS

The links included here were discovered after much of the book was completed. I thought that many of these sites were SO good that I wanted to include them for you as a bonus. They are not sorted or classified but still worth exploring.

Public Domain 4 U

http://www.publicdomain4u.com/

Here is a collection of MP3's of songs that are in the Public Domain. If you like blues, here is a great place to find some classics.

Comments / Notes: _____

_____

_____

Free for Churches

http://freeforchurches.com/taxonomy/term/19

A small collection of links to Public Domain audio sources on the web. There is some great music available through this site.

Comments / Notes: _____

_____

_____

Digital Library for the Decorative Arts and Material Culture

http://digicoll.library.wisc.edu/DLDecArts/

The Digital Library for the Decorative Arts and Material Culture collects and creates electronic resources for study and research of the decorative arts, with a particular focus on Early America. Included are electronic texts and facsimiles, image databases, and Web resources.

Comments / Notes: _____

_____

_____

Digital Book Index

http://www.digitalbookindex.org/index.htm

Digital Book Index provides links to more than 114,000 title records from more than 1800 commercial and non-commercial publishers, universities, and various private sites. About 75,000 of these books, texts, and documents are available free.

Comments / Notes: _____

_____

_____

Gallica: The National Library of France

http://gallica.bnf.fr/

This site has a large collection of classic books and images, but unless you speak French, better run the pages through a page translator.

Comments / Notes: _____

_____

_____

Yale University Beinecke Rare Book and Manuscript Library

http://beinecke.library.yale.edu/dl_crosscollex/

The Beinecke Rare Book & Manuscript Library is Yale University's principal repository for literary papers and for early manuscripts and rare books in the fields of literature, theology, history, and the natural sciences.

Comments / Notes: _____

_____

_____

Liberty Library of Constitutional Classics

http://www.constitution.org/liberlib.htm

The Liberty Library provides a host of electronic texts in html, text or zipped for download. These are primarily classic books and other works on constitutional government, and include works by Plato, Aristotle, Spinoza, Hobbes, Hume, Rousseay and others.

Comments / Notes: _____

_____

_____

Akamac Etexts

http://www.cpm.ll.ehime- u.ac.jp/AkamacHomePage/Akamac_E-text_Links/Akamac_E- text_Links.html

With a focus on texts relevant to the history of economics and social thought, this site provides links arranged in by author in alphabetical order.

Comments / Notes: _____

_____

_____

Etext Archives

http://www.lang.nagoya-u.ac.jp/~matsuoka/e-texts.html
This page seeks to collect any and all e-text archives on the Web.

Comments / Notes: _____
_____
_____

E-Server

http://eserver.org/
The EServer is a growing online community where hundreds of writers, artists, editors and scholars gather to publish works as open archives, available free of charge to readers.

Comments / Notes: _____
_____
_____

University of Kent Online Resources

http://library.kent.ac.uk/library/online/archs.shtml
A nice collection of links to websites containing Public Domain books.

Comments / Notes: _____
_____
_____

Public Domain Torrents

http://www.publicdomaintorrents.com/
Downloads hundreds of Public Domain movies to play on the digital device of your choice.

Comments / Notes: _____
_____
_____

CARRIE

http://www.ku.edu/carrie/
A full text electronic library.

Comments / Notes: _____
_____
_____

Leseratte Library

http://terrenceberres.com/etext.html
A collection of book texts, articles and bibliographies. Also includes links to other Public Domain sites.

Comments / Notes: _____
_____
_____

Wiretap Electronic Text Archive

http://wiretap.area.com/

Wiretap Archive is probably the single useful gopher resource remaining on the Internet. They plan to be considerably expanding their offerings in the near future. More books, more authors.

Comments / Notes: _____

_____

_____

Classic Horror Short Stories

http://www.classichorrorstories.com/

Classic Horror Short Stories (CHSS) borrows the ideas set forth by Project Gutenberg to preserve the world's greatest literature in electronic form. CHSS sets its goal on developing the greatest collection of short stories anywhere.

Comments / Notes: _____

_____

_____

Intellectual Property Information Center

http://www.k-state.edu/academicservices/intprop/pub_domain_materials.htm

Great place to begin searching, not only for Public Domain resources with the links they provide, but also for info about the Public Domain.

Comments / Notes: _____

_____

_____

Federal Citizen Information Center

http://www.pueblo.gsa.gov/

200 publications from the Federal government. Catalog is in the PD, publications listed in the Catalog are usually in the public domain, although it would be a good idea to touch base with the publishing agency if planning to go commercial.

Comments / Notes: _____

_____

_____

Word Max Books

http://www.wordmaxbooks.com

Here you'll find nicely bound booklet reprints of some of the most interesting titles, mostly from the 19th Century. They specialize in military and naval history, tropical travel and geography, and the history of science; but we also have a weakness for general oddities of all sorts, and quirky historical works.

Comments / Notes: _____

_____

_____

CLOSING THOUGHTS

My hope for you in purchasing and using this book is two-fold: First and foremost, I want you to have the adventure of a lifetime. Not only are you reaching back into the heritage of our past, but you are also building upon that foundation. It's a great challenge, privilege and responsibility. It is also an exciting journey back to the past and into the future. Think of it, you have the opportunity to breathe life again into the words spoken by another decades or even centuries ago. How awesome is that?

Second, I want to see you prosper from the information contained in this book. If you do not, it's only because you do not apply the knowledge contained herein. Many of the books in the Public Domain have sold thousands, and in quite a few cases, tens and hundreds of thousands of copies...but here's the rub...those sales were to another generation. People are basically the same at their core. They want the same things, whether the year was 1906 or 2006. Remember that and you will understand the importance of looking back to look forward.

I also want to leave you with a couple final tips and tricks to bear in mind as you discover those treasures. Contained within the treasure you discover may be clues to more treasure. Think about this: Books often contain references and comments in the text that point to other works. Here are some prime clues to keep your eyes open for:

- Bibliographies
- Footnotes
- Ads for other books
- About the author sections
- In-text references to other books and authors

I remember the first time this approach occurred to me...I was reading an old book published in 1910. I was really enjoying it, when all of a sudden, something the author

- 103 -   www.publicdomaincodebook.com

said jumped out at me. He said that so-and-so said in his excellent book...then quoted the author. I sat there for a moment, and then realized that, if the book was being referenced in a book published before 1923, then the referenced book was also in the Public Domain. I know...it seems like a "Duh..." thought, but you might be surprised how many people this would never occur to...perhaps even you! So as you find these treasures, read them and include them as a part of your research. They may be worth more to you than you realize.

One last thing...DO NOT overlook old magazines. If you find a magazine related to your niche that was published in 1922, then, guess what...all the authors of all the articles (not to mention the articles themselves) are in the Public Domain. This is often also true of magazines published in the later years up until 1964. Just be sure to do your copyright research. I remember the first "old" magazine I purchased on Ebay. The find was triggered from a search I was doing for a particular author whose books I love, and whose books are all in the Public Domain. I was doing a search for the author's name on Ebay and had checked the box for searching title and description (this is a great tip). That's when the magazine turned up. The author was a contributor for that issue. I won the auction, and when the magazine arrived, I searched through it and was nearly jumping up and down with excitement. Why? Because it was full of treasure: articles, book reviews, advertisements, quotes, pictures and more...ALL in the Public Domain. I'll be honest with you...this tip is a goldmine in itself. I should have charged extra for it. So definitely include this strategy as a part of your treasure-finding abilities.

In closing...have fun and remember that there is joy in the journey. We all want to prosper, but you might as well have fun doing it, right? Also, don't forget the next bonus section. It's your chance to sharpen your skills as a treasure hunter.

BONUS: CRACK THE CODE!

※

On the following pages, you will find the story *The Old Fisherman's Net*. I wrote this story as a bonus. I wanted to give you a chance at solving a treasure mystery and cracking a real code that will lead to real treasure. The clues you need to solve the numeric puzzle are hidden within the text of the story and within the text of *The Public Domain Code Book*. Some clues may also lead you to other sources as well...or they may not. The numbers included with the story do represent an actual code that reveals the "location" of money awaiting the solver of the puzzle. How much money, you ask? Well, that depends. For every copy of *The Public Domain Code Book* that sells, ten percent (10%) of the total selling price will be placed into a special account. Every time someone purchases a copy of the book, more money is added to the account, also known as the treasure chest. If it takes a while for someone to crack the code, the treasure could literally be worth thousands of dollars! (Don't you think this is much better than some overpriced, worthless bonus?)

How to play. To participate in this adventure, you MUST purchase and own an original copy of the *Public Domain Code Book*...no exceptions. We will verify your purchase using the sales order number you will receive at the time of purchase. Hidden within the text of the *Public Domain Code Book* are clues that will aid you in deciphering the numeric puzzle. It is not easy, but the rewards will be worth it. The message contained in the puzzle reveals instructions on how to stake your claim for the treasure (money) available at the time of "discovery." When the instructions are revealed, you MUST follow them completely. Upon completing all the instructions, you will be notified if you have indeed succeeded in discovering the treasure. You also will be told at that time the amount you "discovered." When an adventurer succeeds in solving the puzzle and follows its instructions, he or she will strike it rich by "discovering" all the money that has accumulated in the special treasure chest (account). As a matter of fact, EVERY time someone solves the puzzle and successfully follows the instructions during the first phase of the adventure (from the product launch until the deadline date listed on the website), he or she will receive the full amount of money available in the chest at that time. Once there is a winner, the chest contents reset to zero.

Then, as new purchases are made, the treasure will increase again according to the sales of the book. If there are a lot of sales and no successful treasure hunter, the amount of money accumulated will be high. If there are two successful puzzle solvers close together, the money awarded will be low. However, you can only win once.

There is a catch. (you knew it, right?) We reserve the right to not reveal to anyone at any time how many books have been sold OR how much money is available to the solver of the puzzle. We also reserve the right to not reveal if anyone has succeeded in solving the puzzle (except to those who do), or how many adventurers have succeeded in solving the puzzle until the date revealed on the special webpage for the contest on the Public Domain Code Book website (www.publicdomaincodebook.com/treasure). On that special treasure page, the names of the successful adventurers will officially be disclosed along with the amounts they "discovered" **after** the deadline date listed on the page. The money "discovered" also will be awarded **on that deadline date**. In the event that there are no solutions offered for the puzzle by the deadline date, clues will be posted on that treasure page as well, and the date will be extended until there is a winner. Clues may also (but not necessarily) offered throughout the treasure hunt to aid you in solving the puzzle.

The adventure will be ongoing. Once this first phase of the adventure is completed on the date listed on the treasure page, the puzzle challenge will be restarted with new treasures. The new treasure available to be discovered will be announced at that time.

Legal Type Stuff. First of all, by participating in the adventure, you signify that you will adhere to all the rules contained herein. Please note that we have taken every precaution to make this a fun and fair adventure.

The successful puzzle solvers will be required to sign non-disclosure contracts or forfeit their discoveries. There also will be no substitutions of any kind (why wouldn't you want the money?) Also, you can only enter the treasure hunt one time per household. Transferring your solution to another person for the purpose of defrauding the treasure hunt will result in the loss of the reward of funds to both parties. Also, entering the treasure hunt under false pretenses in any way (using another person's name, contact info, etc.) will also result in disqualification. In that event, the funds will be returned to the treasure chest to be available for the next puzzle solver.

Please also note. An independant company will be tracking all the sales for the *Public Domain Code Book* to ensure that 10% of EVERY sale is awarded to the solver(s) of the puzzle.

To read the contest rules in their entirety, please go to:

www.publicdomaincodebook.com/contestrules.html

THE OLD FISHERMAN'S NET

❧

Recently I was looking through some old books at one of my favorite used book stores, Wonder Books, when I came across a volume that caught my attention. It was an average-looking old book. There was no fancy cover or guilding on it, unless you consider a tan cloth cover with red block letters for the title to be fancy. I don't normally give a second glance to novels...they're not my "thing." But something seemed familiar about this particular book...like I had read it before or heard about it somewhere...yet I was sure I had never seen it, much less read it.

As I began to flip through the pages, I came across a drawing that really piqued my curiosity. It was an image of the earth wrapped with a fisherman's net. I thought the picture was quite fitting, considering the title of the book, but it still seemed out of place for a book written in 1898. Intrigued, I began to read the preceding page. *Maybe they will mention this net-covered earth in the text*, I thought. Little did I know that what I would read next would challenge my thinking at every level. Here is an excerpt of that text from page 47 of *The Old Fisherman's Net*:

As the old fisherman gathered his fish-filled net back onto the boat, he thought about the story in Scripture where Jesus told Peter to cast his net

1

on the other side of the boat, and how the catch was so great it almost sunk the boat. A grin spread across his face because he knew that he too had been blessed. "Keep pulling, Thomas," he yelled to his grandson. "We're almost done." As the old fisherman looked at all the fish flopping in his net, his mind drifted back once more to the old Bible stories and the parallels Jesus drew between fish and men. "Fishers of men," he thought. "We are all connected in more ways than we realize."

I was really curious now. I had shared that old man's thought with so many others as well. *We are all connected in more ways than we realize.* I continued to read.

The old fisherman and his grandson settled into the boat's cabin for supper. It had been an exciting day of catching fish and they were tired. But now it was time to enjoy some of the fruits of their labor—fresh fish. As they sat there, quietly eating, the old fisherman watched his grandson, proud of the young man he had become. "I think it's time he learns about the secret," he mused as he drank the last of his coffee. Yes, it was time.

"Thomas, I have a secret to tell you," he began. "A secret that was told to me by my grandfather when I was about your age."

"What kind of secret, Grandpa?" Thomas asked.

"Well, Thomas, it's a wonderful secret about buried treasure and the future of the world."

What the heck?! Secrets? Buried treasure? The future of the world? *Well,* I thought, *it IS a novel after all. Authors always wrote about stuff like this.* And I admit, I have always been a sucker for a good treasure hunt.

Revealing the Secret

Since I didn't really have to BE anywhere, I found an empty chair over in the corner of the store, sat down, and continued on with the story.

Thomas's face lit up with excitement. "You found a buried treasure, Grandpa?" The old fisherman chuckled. He had found a treasure, yes, but not the kind Thomas was thinking. "No Thomas," he continued, "I'm not talking about an old pirate's treasure. This is something even more special. The secret I want to share with you is about something in the future...a new way of life. It hasn't happened yet, but it will."

I mused, "The secret is 'Buy oil stocks, Thomas'...you'll be a billionaire in no time, especially with gas selling at $3 per gallon these days."

The old fisherman walked over to the old, wooden cupboard in his cabin. Opening the door, he reached in and pulled out an old globe. It didn't have any navigational value to it, but he loved having it there with him. It was his Grandfather's globe and the old fisherman loved to reminisce about the first time he had seen it. It was the night when HIS grandfather told him the secret. Now he was going to continue the heritage.

"Thomas, go up on the deck and bring me one of those nets. I want to show you something." Thomas ran up the ladder, grabbed the net that was full of fish earlier, and headed back down into the warm cabin below. After handing his Grandpa the net, Thomas sat down on the side of his bunk. What could his Grandpa have to share that was SO secret...especially using a globe and a net?

I was curious too.

The old fisherman proceeded to wrap the net around the globe, then sat down on the bunk beside Thomas.

"Thomas, there is coming a day when the entire world will be covered with a net. I know it sounds strange, and I don't understand what it means, but that is the secret my Grandfather told me, and now I want to share it with you."

Thomas felt a bit disappointed and somewhat confused. "Maybe Grandpa was working too hard today in catching all those fish. After all, he is pretty old, he thought."

"Do you have any questions Thomas?" the old fisherman asked.

"I do have a couple questions, Grandpa...actually, lots of questions," Thomas responded. "How can you put a net around the whole earth? And, what is the net for? And, where did your Grandfather hear such a strange story? And..."

"Hold on just a minute, Thomas," the old fisherman said, laughing. "Let's take these one at a time. First of all, I don't know how you would put a net around the entire earth. I thought it sounded as strange as you do, but I believed my Grandfather and what he shared. Perhaps it would help you understand things a little better if I explained how he learned the secret. Okay?"

"Okay," said Thomas. "I was wondering that anyway."

The old fisherman began, "When my grandfather was around your age, he fell deathly ill. His parents didn't think he would live. For several days he had a high fever and was in a coma. Then a miracle happened...one morning he awoke completely well. It was as if he had never been sick. But he had changed...he was different."

4

"How was he different, Grandpa? What happened to him?"

Well, during the time he was sick with the fever, he had an experience where he saw many things, kind of like a vision I suppose. He left this earth and was shown what would happen in the future."

"You mean he went to heaven?"

"I guess you could call it that, Thomas. I just know what he told me. And what he said was that he went somewhere else and saw many incredible things. When he woke up completely well, he knew things that didn't make sense. He remembered pictures that were confusing to him."

"And the globe in the net was one of those pictures?"

"Yes, Thomas, it was. But he also remembered something about the net itself. He was told that the knots tied in the net represented connecting places, gathering places, for for all kinds of knowledge. And as you can see, Thomas, the knots from the net cover the globe."

Thomas fingered a knot in the net curiously. "What kind of knowledge would you find at those spots, Grandpa?"

The old fisherman looked down at the globe, then looked straight into Thomas's eyes. "I asked my Grandfather that same question. He said he was told that the knowledge found at the knots would represent the wisdom of the ages...secrets from the foundations of the earth. He said that people would be able to find answers to all sorts of questions on any subject they could think of."

My mind was racing. *This guy is describing the Internet...in 1898! He's talking about 'The Net.' Wait a minute...is this a novel, or did the author really have some sort of "visitation" or something?* I also wondered if he gave up any more "secrets." I started to flip through the pages. *Show me something, Grandpa. Give me a clue to what you have up your sleeve.* Bingo! At page 112 I stopped in total shock at what I saw. It was a page of numbers...rows and rows of numbers. "It's a code!" I exclaimed aloud. But a code to what? I started scanning the previous page for a clue about "the code." "There...in the middle of page 110. Tell me what it is, Grandpa!

Just then, the old fisherman pulled an old, folded-up piece of paper from his shirt pocket and handed it to Thomas. "I want to show you this, Thomas. It's a key to unlocking the secret of the net."

"It doesn't look like a key...what's on it?"

"Open it up...carefully...and find out for yourself."

Thomas slowly unfolded the yellowed paper. The edges were frayed and obviously worn with age. Thomas could tell that it had been opened and folded many times before this one...his FIRST time. As he gently opened the paper, it yielded a new mystery: The paper was covered from top to bottom and from left to right with numbers, all in perfect rows and columns.

"They're numbers!" Thomas exclaimed. "What do they mean, Grandpa? Tell me what they mean!"

The old fisherman looked down at the paper, then up at Thomas. "I don't know what they mean, Thomas. Grandfather never told me because he didn't know either. All he remembered was the numbers."

"Where did he see the numbers?"

"They were written on a parchment he was handed while he was at that other place. The voice told him to memorize the numbers because they were the key to the secrets of the universe and to great wealth."

"Great wealth?" Thomas asked.

Great wealth? I echoed silently. What is this book? Who is this author? And why am I sitting here reading this...right here, right now? The whole story seemed so strangely familiar, yet I KNEW I had never seen this book before. I WAS connected to this book though...somehow. It was beginning to seem as if all the forces of the Universe were working together to connect me to it. But why? I was even starting to wonder if I hadn't actually found the book at all, but that the book had instead found me. I know that sounds very "Twilight Zone," but I can't think of a better way to describe it. *Let's see if the old fisherman can shed any more light on this wealth.*

"Yes, Thomas...that is what Grandfather told me...great wealth."

"So why haven't you figured out what the numbers mean, Grandpa? Why haven't you discovered the great wealth?"

"Thomas...I am an old man now, but I devoted my entire life to figuring out the meaning of those numbers. It's actually why I became a fisherman. I figured that since a fishing net was used in the picture Grandfather saw, maybe the answer was somehow related to fishing. I even thought that perhaps the numbers were navigational coordinates that would take me right to where the wealth was hidden, but they haven't. I do not know anymore about the numbers today than I did 60 years ago. So now it's your turn, Thomas. It is up to you to figure out the meaning of the numbers."

"Can't you give me anymore hints, Grandpa?" Thomas asked, feeling quite overwhelmed.

"I've told you all I know...all my Grandfather told me," the old fisherman responded. "He said he was told the numbers reveal a location...coordinates on where to find great wealth and the secrets of the universe. That's all I know, Thomas. Are you up for the challenge?"

Thomas nodded solemnly, "I will figure this out, Grandpa...I promise!"

"Good, Thomas...very good. I know you will. Why don't we turn in for the night? We have another big day ahead of us tomorrow."

"All right, Grandpa," Thomas reponded, knowing full well he would not be sleeping much...he would be thinking about the numbers...

I bought the book and headed home. I, like Thomas, could not stop thinking about the numbers. What did they mean? What do they represent? Do they really lead to great wealth, or is the book really just a novel? Time would tell.

Wondrous wealth welcomes worthy warriors
who win wisdom within the web.

357	623	2041	71	1042	427	1304	781	203	2228
1547	680	19	396	268	530	1694	2415	1248	939
611	3642	1842	3101	2577	1983	2370	891	2966	1901
1171	3337	1362	3483	768	2691	2886	2064	3001	719
1532	1177	26	3919	3203	2147	2677	3243	1418	4507
108	2736	3093	2010	3920	1728	3511	1961	316	1124
2127	3660	4020	3043	1858	999	1987	3701	2278	1778
2049	3138	2257	1588	3534	4121	4537	804	1717	2116
3222	2171	469	2994	43	1285	2438	3363	4367	2022
2854	3278	2806	1189	968	2770	2062	3115	1844	2044
4122	3933	3726	2719	3556	1633	2675	4437	3961	423
2302	2038	4216	1711	879	3154	2334	2642	4223	3016

I hope this story has inspired you to search for the "Great Wealth" that was referred to in the story. The first step to staking your claim is to solve the puzzle. Follow the clues in both the story and throughout the Public Domain Code Book to begin your journey.

Additional clues and hints will be available from time to time at the following related blog sites:

The Public Domain Blog

www.publicdomainblog.com

(This blog is where you will find the latest information on the release of "The Public Domain Code Book.)

&

Spiritual Genetics

www.spiritualgenetics.com

(Spiritual Genetics is the home for my discussion of "stranger than fiction" revelations connected with the story, "The Old Fisherman's Net." What I did not realize at the time I wrote the story, was that there may be more to this story than I realized...it actually might be literally connected to my past...strange as that may seem. Through this blog, I will be presenting the "evidence" so you can decide for yourself whether there is such as a thing as "Spiritual Genetics.")

APPENDIX A

❖

Copyright Exceptions with Public Domain Materials

- *Copyrighted Elements in Public Domain Resources*
- *Privacy and Publicity Rights*
- *Trademarks*
- *Licensing Restrictions*

Copyrighted Portions in Public Domain Resources

There are instances where certain elements of a resource may be in the Public Domain, but other elements are not. An example of this would be the television program, *The Beverly Hillbillies*. Some of the show's episodes are now in the public domain; however, the theme music is protected by copyright. One approach that some businesses have used in this situation is to remove the protected music and provide different, royalty-free music in its place. The most important point here is to do your research homework! I have included copies of all the U.S. Copyright information on the resource disc so that you can be certain your product truly exists in the Public Domain.

Privacy and Publicity Rights

"Privacy and publicity rights reflect separate and distinct interests from copyright interests. Patrons desiring to use materials from this website bear the responsibility of making individualized determinations as to whether privacy and publicity rights are implicated by the nature of the materials and how they may wish to use such materials.

"While copyright protects the copyright holder's property rights in the work or intellectual creation, privacy and publicity rights protect the interests of the person(s) who may be the subject(s) of the work or intellectual creation. Issues pertaining to privacy and publicity may arise when a researcher contemplates the use of letters, diary entries, photographs or reportage in visual, audio, and print formats found in library collections. Because two or more people are often involved in the work (e.g., photographer and subject, interviewer and interviewee) and because of the ease with which various media in digital format can be reused, photographs, audio files, and motion pictures represent materials in which issues of privacy and publicity emerge with some frequency.

"The distinctions among privacy rights, publicity rights, and copyright are best illustrated by example, as follows: An advertiser wishes to use a photograph for a print advertisement. The advertiser approaches the photographer, who holds the copyright in the photograph, and negotiates a license to use the photograph. The advertiser also is required to determine the relationship between the photographer and the subject of the photograph. If no formal relationship (e.g., a release form signed by the subject) exists that permits the photographer to license the use of the photograph for all uses or otherwise waives the subject's, sitter's or model's rights, then the advertiser must seek permission from the subject of the photograph because the subject has retained both privacy and publicity rights in the use of their likeness. The privacy right or interest of the subject is personal in character, that the subject and his/her likeness not be cast before the public eye without his/her consent, the right to be left alone. The publicity right of the subject is that their image may not be commercially exploited without his/her consent and potentially compensation.

"While copyright is a federally protected right under the United States Copyright Act, with statutorily described fair use defenses against charges of copyright infringement, neither privacy nor publicity rights are the subject of federal law. Note also that while fair use is a defense to copyright infringement, fair use is not a defense to claims of violation of privacy or publicity rights. Privacy and publicity rights are the subject of state laws. While many states have privacy and/or publicity laws, others do not recognize such rights or recognize such rights under other state laws or common law legal theories such as misappropriation and false representation. What may be permitted in one state may not be permitted in another. Note also that related causes of action may be pursued under the federal Lanham Act, 15 U.S.C. § 1125 (a), for example, for unauthorized uses of a person's identity in order to create a false endorsement.

"While an individual's right to privacy generally ends when the individual dies, publicity rights associated with the commercial value connected with an individual's name, image or voice may continue. For example, many estates or representatives of famous authors, musicians, actors, photographers, politicians, sports figures, celebrities, and other public figures continue to control and license the uses of those figures' names, likenesses, etc."*

An example of this would be where you have located a Public Domain resource that contains a photograph of Elvis. Because of Publicity Rights held by his estate, you cannot use any likeness of Elvis for commercial gain, even if it is in the Public Domain.

*(Library of Congress website; http://memory.loc.gov/ammem/copothr.html, accessed 1/26/06)

Trademarks

Another area to be careful in when it comes to using Public Domain materials, especially images, movies and music, is the area of trademarks. It is possible to find resources that are in the Public Domain but are still protected by trademark. A good example of this would be an ad advertising Coca-Cola from a 1922 magazine. The magazine may be in the Public Domain, but Coca-Cola retains the trademark control of their brand.

Licensing Restrictions

There are situations where a resource may be in the Public Domain but its use may still be limited due to licensing restrictions. This is where the owner of the Public Domain piece—a painting for instance—has the right to limit access to the piece, even though it is in the Public Domain. Attorney Stephen Fishman provides greater insight into this in his excellent book, *The Public Domain*:

"Theoretically, once a work of art enters the public domain it can be copied freely by anyone for any use. However, to make a copy you must first have access to the original. And here lies the problem: Owners of works of art in the public domain are under no obligation to give anyone access to copy the work. Even when a work of art is in the public domain, the canvas, marble, clay, or other physical substance in which it is embodied is still owned by somebody—whether a museum, gallery, or private collector. Since a work of art is a piece of personal property as well as a work of authorship, the owner enjoys all the rights of any personal property owner. Copyright protection may expire or never exist in the first place, but personal property rights attach to all works of art and last forever.

"Private owners of public domain works of art are under no obligation to allow anyone into their home to make copies of the art or even to view it. And most major museums in the United States restrict the public from taking photographs of their collections."

"If you want a high-quality publishable photograph or other copy of a painting or other artwork, you must ask the museum to provide you with one. You will be charged a fee for this and usually required to sign a license agreement restricting how you may use the photograph or other copy. Such licensing fees are a major source of income for many art museums. Moreover, many museums will not agree to license their works for products that might compete with their own products, such as calendars and note cards."

(Fishman, Stephen, *The Public Domain: How to Find & Use Copyright-Free Writings, Music, Art & More* (Berkeley, CA: Nolo, 2004), 160-161.)

APPENDIX B

Types of Source Materials in the Public Domain

When many talk about the Public Domain, they usually limit their discussions to books, images and movies. But there is MUCH more amazing "stuff" that is actually in the Public Domain. Here is a fairly complete listing of the different types of "information" items that are out there awaiting discovery. There are even a few things on this list you would have probably never considered to be in the Public Domain (like "nature").

Advertising Trade Cards

Alphabets, Numbers & Symbols

Ancient Art

Ancient Writings / Artifacts

Audio Recordings

Blueprints

Books

Broadsides

Calendars

Calligraphy

Catalogs

Cigarette Cards

Clothing Patterns

Comic Books

Diaries

Documents / Charters (Governmental)

Engineering / Technical Drawings

Fabric

Films

Children's Game Ephemera (Boxes, Playing Pieces, etc.)

Genealogies

Gift Wrap

Greeting Cards

Herbal / Home / Medicinal Remedies

Hymnals

Journals

Labels (Cans, Fruit Crates, Tobacco Boxes, Bottles, etc.)

Letters

Magazines

Manuals

Maps

Menus

Money (Obsolete)

Movies

Musical Scores

Nature

Newsletters

Newspapers

Oral Traditions

Original Art

Packaging

Paper Dolls

Passenger Logs (Trains, Ships, etc.)

Periodicals

Petroglyphs

Photographs

Pictographs

Playbills

Playing Cards

Plays / Movie Scripts

Postcards

Posters

Programs

Puzzles

Recipes

Record Albums

Song Lyrics

Speeches

Sports Cards

Stamps

Wallpaper

Valentines

APPENDIX C

20+ Ways to Find Public Domain Materials Offline

Much of this book is focused on doing your Public Domain research online. The most obvious reason for this is that it's easy to sit at your computer and "travel all over the world" with the click of a mouse. However, in order to find some items, you're going to have to do your research the old-fashioned way...look for it offline.

I've put together a list of over twenty places to dig around for those lost gems. Yes, it takes longer to do this type of research, but for me, it's also much more enjoyable. I guess it's the thrill of the hunt...something I love. So in your rush for find the next million-dollar idea from the Public Domain, MAKE SURE to refer to this list.

1. Bookstores
2. Used Bookstores
3. Flea Markets
4. Antique Shops
5. Thrift / Goodwill Stores
6. Estate Sales
7. Public Auctions
8. Auction Houses
9. Garage / Yard Sales
10. Libraries
11. Library Sales
12. Historical Societies
13. Book / Literary Clubs
14. Book Shows
15. Antiques Shows
16. Published Bibliographies
17. Encyclopedias
18. Grandma and Her Friends

More on next page...

19. Other Public Domain Books
    a. Ads for Other Books
    b. Other Books by Author
    c. Recommended Reading
    d. Bibliography
    e. Author References Within the Text
    f. Footnotes

20. Old Magazines
    a. Articles
    b. Ads
    c. Book Reviews
    d. Author References Within the Text
    e. Book Excerpts

21. Newspapers
    a. Articles
    b. Ads
    c. Book Reviews
    d. Author References Within the Text
    e. Book Excerpts

APPENDIX D

⸎

Public Domain Niche Categories—Discovering Your Niche

In developing products, there are a few things you can always count on...People always love: Information, How-to guides, Nostalgia and the Classics. Keep these points in mind when looking for potential markets to develop information products for. That being said, you also need to remember that just because you think something is cool doesn't necessarily mean everyone else will. It is seldom a wise decision to develop a product first, and then go out to find customers willing to buy it. The only way to truly be successful in developing and selling information products is to follow this simple 3-step rule:

1. Find a group of passionate people with money to spend, and who will spend it compulsively.

2. Determine exactly what it is they want.

3. Give them what they want.

Follow that process and success will likely be kicking down your door. Don't follow that process and success may be difficult to come by. Let's look at each point a little more in depth.

1. Find a group of passionate people with money to spend, and who will spend it compulsively.

You know people like this, partly because this may describe you, when it comes to something you love. Here are some topic examples that are considered "evergreen", meaning, there will always be a market in these areas...let's see if one strikes a chord with you:

- Making money

- Astrology and the occult

- Health (herbs, botanical remedies, natural cures, etc.)

- Cooking

- Magic

- Exercise and fitness

- Handicrafts

- Beauty

- Sex

- Psychology

- Investing

- Losing weight

(Source: The Accumulated Wisdom of Mail Order: What Sells and What Doesn't, A Thirty Year Record, by Eugene M. Schwartz)

2. Determine exactly what it is they want

What passion do you spend YOUR money on? Why? What one thing would YOU love to have connected with that passion? Do you following the logic here? Good!

I recently purchased a poster from a vendor on eBay who makes an "art" out of selling Public Domain content. (pun intended). This poster was of an old ad for the Santa Fe Railroad, and it brought together many of my passions... it featured an awesome image of a Native American chief (my family is Cherokee), it was a train advertisement (I have loved trains since I was little boy), it was a Public Domain piece (which is cool since I was working on this project), it was a classic art piece (I am an artist and love classic design) and the price was right (always a good thing). The vendor was able to provide me with exactly what I was looking for. More importantly, he is also providing exactly what many others are looking for as well. He does quite nicely with eBay sales every day, and he does it almost exclusively with Public Domain images! Beautiful!

Now, perhaps you are thinking that since this person is selling specific Public Domain images on eBay, it wouldn't be worth your while to do so as well. Competition can be good. Just because there is a dominant vendor in an industry doesn't mean that others should resist competing with them. Competition actually encourages new ideas and strategies, which can lead to brilliant new ideas. And think about it...you see this play out daily in nearly every arena of sales—from automobiles and burgers to clothing airplane tickets. So don't be afraid to jump into the fray! However, creating original products will always keep you ahead of the game.

Here are 15 niche areas to consider:

1) **Sports**
   a. Hunting / Fishing
   b. Professional Sports
   c. Olympics
   d. Games

2) **Food**
   a. Recipes
   b. Diets
   c. Herbs
   d. Gardening

3) **Health**
   a. Herbal Cures
   b. Personal Care
   c. Studies
   d. Exercise

4) **Arts**
   a. Collections
   b. Postcards
   c. How To Books
   d. Framed Prints

5) **Religion**
   a. Classic Writings
   b. Self-Help
   c. Classic Images
   d. Collections of Quotes

6) **Environment**
   a. Field Guides
   b. Living Off the Land
   c. Caring for the Environment
   d. Reports

7) **Hobbies**
   a. Collections
   b. Antiques
   c. Photo Books
   d. Scrapbooking

8) **Clothing**
   a. Old Catalogs
   b. Patterns
   c. Trends
   d. Fabrics

9) **Poetry**
   a. Collections
   b. Complete Works
   c. Posters
   d. T-Shirts / Mugs

10) **Transportation**
   a. Cars
   b. Bicycles
   c. Boats
   d. Motorcycles

11) **History**
   a. Civil War
   b. Ancient Civilizations
   c. Native Americans
   d. Dinosaurs

12) **Technology**
   a. Facts Guides
   b. Novelties
   c. Studies
   d. How To Guides

13) **Animals**
   a. Pet Care
   b. Pet Guides
   c. Hunting Techniques
   d. Framed Prints

14) **Music**
   a. History
   b. Musical Instruments
   c. Classic Recordings
   d. Ethnic Styles

15) **Government**
   a. Historic Acts
   b. Conspiracies
   c. Maps
   d. Famous Documents

3. Give them what they want

This is the easy part. Once you have identified exactly what your niche wants, give it to them. How hard is that? Of course, you have to develop the product depending on what you decide to sell to your niche. If the thought of product creation scares you, don't sweat it, there are many experts out there who can easily create it for you according to YOUR specs and desires. For more information on pursuing this approach, check out places like www.elance.com, www.scriptlance.com, www.guru.com and others.

APPENDIX E

❦

Case Studies in Developing and Using Public Domain Content

CASE STUDY #1

Dover Publications
http://www.doverpublications.com/

Dover was established in 1941 by Hayward and Blanche Cirker, who managed the company through more than a half-century of growth. Over the years, Dover built a thriving business on making an extraordinarily wide range of intellectual property available to customers with special interests.

In 1951, Dover broke new ground by introducing one of the first trade paperbacks. Until then paperbacks were cheaply produced pocket-sized editions selling in drugstores for 25 cents. Dover produced larger, high-quality paperbacks and sold them in bookstores for a dollar or more. While competitors initially predicted disaster, they soon recognized the strong market response and got on the bandwagon.

Since their founding, Dover Publications has built their reputation by offering remarkable products at amazing prices. They primarily publish books no longer published by their original publishers—often, but not always, books in the public domain. Many of these books are of particular historical interest or high quality.

Dover's policy of cheap (while durable) binding means their books are sold at a low cost. They are well known for their reprints of classic works of literature, classical sheet music and of public-domain images from the 19th century. They also publish an extensive collection of mathematical, scientific and engineering texts.

THE PUBLIC DOMAIN CODE BOOK

Hayward Cirker, co-founder of Dover Publications once said, "We can take a book on an esoteric subject and sell more copies of it than anyone believed possible." This explains why the New York Times would say, "The shelves of American bookstores, not to mention those of millions of book lovers, would look very different if not for Cirker's influence."

Dover's offerings include a vast range of subjects such as American History, Americana, Folklore, Mythology, Children's Classics, Cookbooks, Nutrition, Literature, Nature, Puzzles, Gardening and dozens of other subjects, now with over 8,000 books available.

In keeping with their mission to provide classic resources at reasonable prices, they are utilizing nearly every primary form of information content for Public Domain from books and clip art books and CD's to posters and music CD's.

You will find Dover's product line online, but they also continue to maintain print catalog sales. You will also find many of their products in retail bookstores like Borders and Barnes and Nobel as well as specialty stores and gift shops. This company has made an art out of using Public Domain materials and should be an inspiration to anyone with a passion for classic media products.

Here are a few examples of the thousands of Public Domain offerings from Dover Publications.

Dover Publications
31 East 2nd Street
Mineola, NY 11501-3852
Fax: 516-742-6953

CASE STUDY #2

A2ZCDS

http://www.a2zcds.com/

A2ZCDS is the world's largest and fastest growing innovative multi-media library. Through its vast and unique distribution network, the company provides historical and educational CDs and DVDs covering thousands of topics to every corner of the globe. The ceaseless research and polling process at A2ZCDS constantly identifies and responds to existing and emergent areas of interests.

They are amongst the pioneers in restoring, preserving and immortalizing audiovisual media content in CD and DVD formats. This involves an ever-ongoing quest for product excellence. At the end of these efforts a wide range of clients—academic scholars, scientific and historical researchers as well as movie aficionados—are benefited by A2ZCDS research and development in innovation. Mentioned below are some of the company's most popular audiovisual products:

HISTORICAL CDs

The past unfolds in graphic detail right before your eyes. A2ZCDS has catalogued popular areas of research and general interest that range from the earliest American settlers, key historical personages and national evolution to manned space flights. The CDs are designed and mapped for complete user-friendliness, requiring virtually no computer skills to explore. Each historical CD from A2ZCDS includes extensive information on that particular subject, including illustrations, film clips, historic photographs and documents, maps, etc. in easy-to-read PDF format. The historical CD range from A2ZCDS has won wide acclaim for its imaginativeness in selection of material, the sheer volume of content and the care with which it is categorized and presented. Several leading authorities on American history have extended their appreciation and regular patronage of these invaluable research tools. A2ZCDS historical CDs are also primary, choice reference material for those with a more casual interest in matters of historical importance.

VINTAGE MOVIE DVDs

The best of the previous century's movies are often, sadly, no longer available through conventional market sources. Since these constitute an integral part of our cultural heritage, A2ZCDS has launched a massive initiative by offering the widest-ever range of rare vintage movies in DVD format. These timeless gems of the silver screen have been scientifically restored, re-mastered and formatted for the best possible viewing experience.

Never before has such an extensive selection of vintage cinema been presented on the market. The customer response has been both thought-provoking and intensely gratifying—it has become evident that there has been a dearth of quality movies from the past that had, so far, not been addressed effectively. Vintage movie DVDs from A2ZCDS are amongst the most popular and fastest-selling products in the company's inventory.

DOCUMENTARY DVDs

The world as we know it. The world as it was. The world as it will be. These media offer an astounding amount of information on any imaginable topic, sourced from the world's leading authorities and information banks. Documentary film clips of heritage in the making. Landmark cultural events. World-changing concepts, discoveries and inventions. If there is any information anywhere in the world on any of the subjects covered in these treasure-chests of knowledge, they contain in. Catalogued, indexed, categorized—and authenticated by all relevant official sources. These DVDs make for limitless hours of fascinating learning experience.

As a result of constant innovation, exemplary products and outstanding customer service, A2ZCDS is quickly becoming a household name. It numbers amongst the most trusted, efficient and user-friendly sources of educational and entertainment media on the market today. They've sold over 250,000 CDs to date.

A2ZCDS.com
1618 Camerbur Dr. Orlando, FL 32805, USA
Phone: 1-866-254-8579, Fax: 1-954-337-6215
E-mail: support@a2zcds.com

CASE STUDY #3

Pat O'Brien & Joe Vitale / Pelmanism
http://www.pelmanismonline.com/

Pat O'Brien was digging around in a back-hills Texas shop and discovered some old magazines from the 1920's. They were in decent condition so he decided to buy them. He thought of his good friend Dr. Joe Vitale and how much he would probably love them. So Pat brought the magazines to their Mastermind group meeting. Joe was flipping through the magazines, using the old ads to give the group an impromptu marketing lesson. That's when Joe came across an advertisement for Pelmanism. It was like time stood still. Finally, Joe spoke: "I've heard of Pelmanism." Joe was excited and his excitement led to a quest to locate the books.

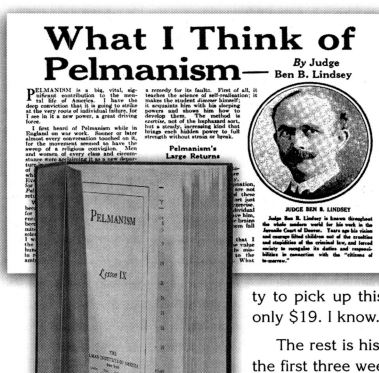

After a few weeks of searching, Pat found a mint copy of the 1919 books for sale—all 12 of them. Everything was there. Everything...including the secrets to how the huge fortunes of the 1920's were created. After spending 6 hours scanning the books and converting them into PDF's, Pat and Joe put up a website and sent out an e-mail about their discovery to their lists. They were given their customers the opportunity to pick up this excellent course from the past for only $19. I know...I got mine!

The rest is history...they sold 1,465 copies sold in the first three weeks...that's $27,385 in 21 days. This is one great example of what is possible with public domain materials.

Pat O'Brien & Joe Vitale / Pelmanism
http://www.pelmanismonline.com/

CASE STUDY #4

The Titanic Historical Society, Inc.
http://www.titanichistoricalsociety.org/

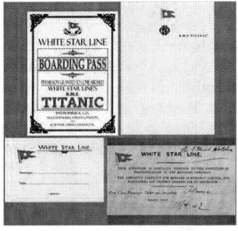

The possibilities available with Public Domain materials are limited only by imagination and the ability to locate PD materials within your niche. And the numbers of niche markets that one could focus on are as numerous as the materials themselves. In this case study, we see an excellent example of a group focused on an extremely small niche market and their vast use of Public Domain Materials: The Titanic Historical Society.

The Titanic Historical Society, Inc. (THS) is the premier information source for all things Titanic and White Star Line related. Formed in 1963, the THS was the first and is the largest global organization dedicated to preserving the history of RMS Titanic and the White Star Line. They host the Titanic Museum, a unique collection of personal items donated by survivors and their families, historical documents and memorabilia from Titanic, Olympic, Britannic and White Star Line ships. They also offer the opportunity to purchase Titanic collectibles and mementos through their online Museum Shop.

A trip to their website and their Museum Shop reveals a fantastic assortment of products utilizing Public Domain materials, from books and booklets to menus and tickets, many of which were produced for them by 7C's Press. The website also features reproductions of classic postcards, newspapers, blueprints, brochures, recordings and many other "paper" products, demonstrating their ability to recognize demand for different types of products within this special niche. This has really positioned them as "the premier source" for all things Titanic. Of course, a blockbuster movie and the actual discovery of the Titanic have helped ad fuel to their passionate fire! (Take note on this point). They truly exhibit the amazing possibilities available in successfully developing Public Domain materials.

APPENDIX F

❈

Catalog of U.S. Government Publications (CGP): Search Tips

The Catalog of U.S. Government Publications provides an index to print and electronic publications created by Federal agencies. When available, links are provided to the full-text of these publications. Additionally, the locate libraries feature enables users to find libraries by state or area code that can make print publications available for their use. Coverage is January 1994 - April 2005.

The Catalog uses WAIS database search software that provides several search options. There are fielded searches and search terms may be combined by using Boolean logic. Using either or both of these features yields more precise search results. The more specific the query is defined, the more relevant the search results will be. However, if unfamiliar with how records are formatted or how the search mechanism works, a query can be too specific and yield no results.

FORMULATING SEARCHES

Begin by choosing the terms you wish to search. A search term may be words, initials, or numbers. Search terms can be subject terms; an author's, editor's, or organization's name; words in a title or series; geographic terms; format terms (such as computer file, database, microfiche, video recording, etc.); or identifying numbers or dates.

Once the search terms are identified, they should be entered in the appropriate field or combination of fields. For most users the keyword or title search will be sufficient. The entire bibliographic record is searched when a keyword is used. This is a much broader search, and likely to produce more results than a title search which only searches the title field of the record. Searching fields is recommended particularly when looking for a known item.

STOPWORDS

Like many database search systems, the WAIS search mechanism employs the use of "stop words." These are common words that the system ignores, therefore they do not have to be included in a search string. The CGP stopword list includes only 10 words.

adj and for nor the an as from or to

SAMPLE SEARCHES

1. Search for Online Titles

Use the Keyword search (online titles) function to create a subset of the CGP that only includes titles available online. Include PURL or http as part of your search strategy. Combine this with strategies described in the BASIC SEARCHING section to locate topical information. This strategy can also be used with the name of a Government agency or to conduct numerical searches, but only records for online titles will be retrieved.

2. Search by Agency Name

Search for agencies from the Keyword Search option. Enter the query as a phrase containing significant words from the agency name. "The" and "of" are stopwords and are not necessary to enter. Department, when part of a title of a work, is always spelled out. In all other instances (e.g., publishing agency or subject) it is abbreviated as dept. The order in which terms are entered affects results. Entering "state dep*" will not retrieve the entries for the Department of State. If you are unsure of the correct word order, enter a search string with both options: "state dept" OR "dept state".

Since an agency publishes many different titles, it is helpful to include one or more subject terms as well as the agency name. For example, to search for publications on post traumatic stress disorder issued by the Department of Veterans Affairs, enter the keyword query:

"dept. veterans affairs" AND "post traumatic stress"

3. Search by Report Number

Search for publications by report number and other identifying numbers by enclosing the complete number to be searched in quotation marks.

Report Number Examples: "EPA/600/R-94/038a" "JPL 400-363" "Serial no. 105-87"

Accession and Order Number Examples: "ED 331282" "N 92-22208" "PB 93-100048"

Contract and Grant Number Examples: "DE-AC07-761D01" "A63972" "307-51-08-04"

Quotation marks are also effective in searching for publications by other kinds of numbers including: series, task, project, and International Standard Book Numbers (ISBN).

4. Search by Title

It is not necessary to know the exact title of a Government information product to use the title field. Results will display records with the search terms anywhere within the title field. Boolean logic, phrase searching, and other basic search techniques described above can be used in the title field. When a keyword search results in too many records, using the title search is a viable alternative. For example, a keyword search of drug* AND teen* resulted in 78 hits, while producing only 5 as a title search.

5. Search by SuDoc (Superintendent of Documents) Class Number

The Superintendent of Documents (SuDoc) number is the call number scheme used in depository libraries for their Federal documents collections. Because this classification scheme arranges materials by the authoring agency and type of publication, a SuDoc number fielded search allows one to locate similar resources by an agency. At least up to the stem of the SuDoc number must be entered for the search to be executed properly. The stem includes the initial letters and numbers up to and including the colon (:). Be sure to insert a space between letters and numbers unless there is intervening punctuation. No spaces precede or follow symbols. Do not use quotation marks (" ") in a SuDoc field search. For example:

EP 1.2:B 74/2 retrieves the specific document: Read this if you plan to breathe this summer : advisory for those with asthma breathing problems and for children, older adults, and people who work outdoors.

EP 1.2: retrieves other general publications from the Environmental Protection Agency.

For a more information about the SuDoc classification system see *An Explanation of the Superintendent of Documents Classification System* and the *GPO Classification Manual.*

6. Search by Depository Item Number

Depository item numbers are used to identify categories of publications or specific periodicals, looseleaf services, and other continuing publications selected by Federal depository libraries for their collections. Item numbers can be used to find a particular kind of publication issued by a Federal agency. It also may be used as a tool to assist depository librarians refine their item selections.

An example of a Depository Item Number is: 1008-D. Information in parentheses following an item number identifies that the item is available in microfiche (MF), paper (P), electronic (E), or online (Online). It is not necessary to use these in the search string, but if used, the parentheses must be omitted.

7. Search by GPO Stock Number

The GPO sales stock number is a unique twelve digit number assigned to each item available for sale by the Superintendent of Documents, U.S. Government Printing Office. An example of a GPO Stock Number is: 030-001-00168-7. When using this field to search, do not enclose the stock number in quotations. Only if the stock number is used in the via keyword search in combination with other search terms, should the number be enclosed in quotation marks.

8. Search by Publication Date

The publication date field can be used to limit a search to information published in a specific year or for a range of years. Remember, although the database contains records created since January 1994, there may be publications with earlier publication dates. The field appears as:

Publication date search:

<u>1900</u> TO <u>2100</u>

Simply enter the date range, using four digits for the year, to conduct a publication date search. To find publications issued in single year, put the date in both date fields. For example, if the publication year is 1994, use [1994] to [1994]. Do not leave either date field blank, doing so will produce an inexact search result.

9. Search by Cataloging Date

The cataloging date search can be used to limit search results to titles cataloged during a specific time period. The <005> field of a MARC record is the cataloging date and time stamp and appears in this sample as:

<005> 19990922103100.0

The initial eight numbers refer to the date (yyyy/mm/dd) in which the record was created by GPO. In this case the date is September 22, 1999. The remaining numbers represent the time of day the cataloging record was generated.

When using this search strategy the asterisk (*) must be used after the numeric representation of the date. This truncation alerts the search mechanism to ignore the time stamp numbers in the rest of the <005> string. Please note that use of leading zeros is required for this search, e.g., 09 for September or 08 for the 8th day of a month.

Examples of searches and results:

Search	Result
199909* AND PURL	Cataloging records created in September 1999 for publications available online
199902* AND "Dept. of Justice"	Cataloging records created in February 1999 for Dept. of Justice publications
19990208*	Cataloging records created February 8, 1999
1999020* AND "Dept. of Justice"	Cataloging records created between February 1, 1999 and February 9, 1999 for Dept. of Justice publications

Searching for a wide date range of records will often retrieve too much material for the system to handle. When expecting a number that exceeds the maximum that the the database permits, break down your search into smaller blocks of days:

Search	Result
1998011*	Cataloging records created between January 10, 1998 and January 19, 1998

10. Search by Multiple Fields

To narrow search results and to retrieve more useful records, conduct a multiple field query. Choose from Title, Superintendent of Documents Class Number, Depository Item Number, GPO Sales Stock Number, or Publication Date searches then click the SUBMIT button. A search form that meets your specifications is generated. Once the form is produced, all chosen fields must be used to achieve accurate results. Chosen fields cannot be left blank. Use the search protocols described above for each of the chosen fields.

INTERPRETING RESULTS

Summary Records

The search results lists present a summary record for each publication. The summary record includes the title, format (i.e. microfiche, CD-ROM), date of publication, issuing agency, SuDocs Class Number and [[Depository Item Number]]. If the publication is available online, a direct link is provided. If the title is for sale by GPO, a GPO Stock Number will also be supplied. See the sample below:

> ATF, the youth crime gun interdiction initiative : crime gun trace analysis reports : the illegal youth firearms markets in 17 communities. 1997] United States. T 70.2:C 86. GPO stock no.: 048-012-00106-6. [[0971-B]].
>
> http://www.atf.treas.gov/core/firearms/ycgii/ycgii.htm
>
> Rank: 329 Locate Libraries, Short Record, Full Record

Once a publication is identified, a link is available to locate Federal depository libraries that received that publication. A search for libraries can be conducted by area code or state.

Record Displays

The Short Record provides a user-friendly display with the basic information one needs to locate or cite a source.

The Full Record, on the other hand, provides the complete and detailed MARC21 catalog record for the publication. Both displays have direct links to online versions of the publication if they are available. Looking at the fields in a MARC21 record provides an opportunity to see the record structure which could prove beneficial in refining a search.

http://www.gpoaccess.gov/cgp/index.html (Accessed May 5, 2006)

APPENDIX G

❧

Setting Up an Art Sales Business Using Public Domain Content

Let's say you want to use Public Domain images to start a product business on Ebay that specializes in selling artwork like posters, maps, cards, fine art, etc. You will obviously need to find a cost-effective way to create your products. You COULD take the images to a commercial printer and have them offset printed, but that will cost you a fortune, especially if you want to offer a wide variety of art pieces. You could easily tie up thousands of dollars in producing an inventory that may not even sell. But before you panic at the thought of needing to take out a second mortgage on your home, take a deep breath and allow me to direct your attention to a simple solution—inkjet printers. Using a wide-format inkjet printer is THE answer to getting your art business up and running, quickly and inexpensively.

A trip to Staples or Circuit City will give you a quick education on the different printer manufacturers that are available out there—HP, Lexmark, Epson, Brother, Xerox, Canon, etc. Regardless of what those well-meaning sales people might tell you, my experience and research says that you need to seriously look at the Epson product line of printers first. Sure, there are other great printers out there (I own three HP printers and a Canon or two along with my Epson printers). But Epson has **mastered** the On-Demand delivery concept with their line of excellent printers and inks. As a company, Epson is serious about quality, both in their printers and in the prints their printers produce…and it shows. They have the best software interfaces and printer drivers out there, and their new Ultrachrome K3 inks are fade resistant for over 100 years. (a fact you might want to point out in your sales letter!) thanks in part to the fact that they are pigment-based. Add to that their printers' ability to print on canvas, watercolor paper, archival paper and a host of other mediums and you end up with a winning combination that will not only make your business run efficiently, but also profitable. Gone are the days of expensive, large run offset print runs (unless you find yourself needing thousands of copies of the same image. Then it makes sense). Here is a listing of the latest wide-format printers Epson has to offer *(as of January 2006)*:

Epson Stylus Photo 1280 – *Around $400*

- Prints up to 13" wide
- Superior, 6-color Photo Ink System
- True BorderFree™ photo printing in 6 popular sizes
- Ideal for 12" x 12" scrapbook layouts
- Water-resistant and lightfast[1] media
- USB / Parallel Interface

Epson Stylus Photo R1800 – *Around $550*

- 8-color Epson UltraChrome Hi-Gloss™ pigment inkset for archival-quality glossy and matte photos
- Fade-resistant photos lasting up to 100-200 years[1]
- Output photos up to 13" wide
- Speeds through a 11" x 14" photo in under 2 minutes
- Creates borderless photos in seven popular sizes
- Prints directly on ink jet printable CDs/DVDs
- Built-in fast connectivity with Hi-Speed USB 2.0 and FireWire®

Epson Stylus Pro 4800 – *Around $2,000*

- 17" Wide Desktop Printer
- 8-color Epson UltraChrome K3™ Ink
- Advanced Black & White Printing Technology

Epson Stylus Pro 7800 – *Around $3,000*

- 24" Wide Format Printer
- 8-color Epson UltraChrome K3™ Ink
- Advanced Black & White Printing Technology

Epson Stylus Pro 9800 – *Around $5,000*

- 44" Wide Format Printer
- 8-color Epson UltraChrome K3™ Ink
- Advanced Black & White Printing Technology

Now, if you are a little short on startup cash and want to produce art prints or posters, you still have a few options available to you. The first solution you have is to outsource your print production to a company like Kinkos or Staples. Most of their stores are equipped with large-format printers and can output whatever you need. You will not make the same profits as you might when producing the prints yourself, but this option still enables you to get your prints produced quickly and easily. Make sure you check with your local store to find out what their media requirements and formats are. They may vary store to store.

Another solution for you to consider is to buy a used printer. Ebay is a great place to start looking. This option may be a good way for you to get started until you're making enough money to purchase a new printer. Here are a few pointers to keep in mind when looking for a used printer:

- Do your homework on the printer. Learn what you can about the specific model you're interested in. Go to Google and type in the manufacturer and model...you should find all the information you need to know (such as the types of media it will print on, print sizes, ink costs, networking options, etc).

- Try to find out the printer's history and print count if possible. Sellers often list this if they know it. Don't be afraid to ask them if they don't mention it.

- You will also want to watch out for clogged print heads. The little nozzles in the print heads are smaller than the thickness of a human hair. A lack of care, lack of use, using generic inks, etc can result in clogging the print heads over time. They are a pain to unclog, if you are even able to do so.

- Make sure the printer comes with the necessary parts needed for operation. Add-ons like cables, power cords, print drivers and software, ink cartridges, etc. can add up.

- Make sure your computer is compatible with the requirements of the printer. You do not want to purchase a printer that connects to your computer through a USB port if your computer doesn't have one.

Don't forget to consider earlier models of the latest and greatest printers currently available. You can often find a great printer this way for a fraction of the cost of the "new" model. Take the Epson Stylus 7800 printer, for example...before this model came along, there was the 7600, and before it, the 7500 and before it, the 7000. To give you some perspective on the kind of pricing difference I'm talking about...at the time of this writing (January 2006), there was a "like new" Epson Stylus 7000 with a Postscript RIP available on Ebay for $660. That's an incredible bargain considering the Epson Stylus 7800 with a Postscript RIP will cost you $4,000!

Here's a complete list of Epson's new and older model wide-format printers (17" paper widths and larger)

Stylus Color 1520	Stylus Pro 7000	Stylus Pro 9600
Stylus Color 3000	Stylus Pro 7500	Stylus Pro 9800
Stylus Pro 4000	Stylus Pro 7600	Stylus Pro 10000
Stylus Pro 4800	Stylus Pro 7800	Stylus Pro 10600
Stylus Pro 5000	Stylus Pro 9000	
Stylus Pro 5500	Stylus Pro 9500	

Power User Tip: Print out your Public Domain artwork painting on canvas. Then, using a fine brush and some oil paints, add some highlight details to the painting to compliment and enhance the image. This does NOT require a lot of skill to do. Plus, investing the few extra minutes of work will not only add texture and detail to your print, it will also add perceived value! You can easily increase the selling price (and get it) for your artwork because, now, you are not just selling an art print; you are selling a **custom, hand-embellished gallery print**. Adding this type of embellishment is a pretty common practice in the artist community, so you might as well benefit from this trick of the trade as well!

THE PUBLIC DOMAIN CODE BOOK
WORDSEARCH KEY

STOP!

Only use this key as a last resort.
Knowing where to look takes all the fun out of the search.

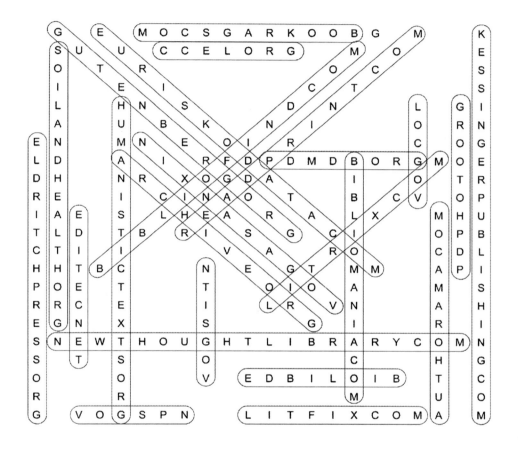

authorama.com	pdphoto.org	gutenberg.org
humanistictexts.org	soilandhealth.org	readprint.com
bibliomania.com	euriskodata.com	editec.net
ccel.org	kessinger-publishing.com	litfix.com
ntis.gov	archive.org	bibliofind.com
loc.gov	biolib.de	bookrags.com
pdmdb.org	litrix.com	eldritchpress.org
nps.gov	newthoughtlibrary.com	nix.nasa.gov

"Books are the treasured wealth of the world and the fit inheritance of generations and nations." —Henry David Thoreau

ⓒopyright
United States Copyright Office

Copyright Basics

What Is Copyright?

Copyright is a form of protection provided by the laws of the United States (title 17, U.S. Code) to the authors of "original works of authorship," including literary, dramatic, musical, artistic, and certain other intellectual works. This protection is available to both published and unpublished works. Section 106 of the 1976 Copyright Act generally gives the owner of copyright the exclusive right to do and to authorize others to do the following:

- To *reproduce* the work in copies or phonorecords;
- To prepare *derivative works* based upon the work;
- *To distribute copies or phonorecords* of the work to the public by sale or other transfer of ownership, or by rental, lease, or lending;
- *To perform the work publicly*, in the case of literary, musical, dramatic, and choreographic works, pantomimes, and motion pictures and other audiovisual works;
- *To display the work publicly*, in the case of literary, musical, dramatic, and choreographic works, pantomimes, and pictorial, graphic, or sculptural works, including the individual images of a motion picture or other audiovisual work; *and*
- In the case of *sound recordings, to perform the work publicly* by means of a *digital audio transmission.*

In addition, certain authors of works of visual art have the rights of attribution and integrity as described in section 106A of the 1976 Copyright Act. For further information, request Circular 40, *Copyright Registration for Works of the Visual Arts.*

It is illegal for anyone to violate any of the rights provided by the copyright law to the owner of copyright. These rights, however, are not unlimited in scope. Sections 107 through 121 of the 1976 Copyright Act establish limitations on these rights. In some cases, these limitations are specified exemptions from copyright liability. One major limitation is the doctrine of "fair use," which is given a statutory basis in section 107 of the 1976 Copyright Act. In other instances, the limitation takes the form of a "compulsory license" under which certain limited uses of copyrighted works are permitted upon payment of specified royalties and compliance with statutory conditions. For further information about the limitations of any of these rights, consult the copyright law or write to the Copyright Office.

Who Can Claim Copyright?

Copyright protection subsists from the time the work is created in fixed form. The copyright in the work of authorship *immediately* becomes the property of the author who created the work. Only the author or those deriving their rights through the author can rightfully claim copyright.

In the case of works made for hire, the employer and not the employee is considered to be the author. Section 101 of the copyright law defines a "work made for hire" as:

1 a work prepared by an employee within the scope of his or her employment; or

2 a work specially ordered or commissioned for use as:
   - a contribution to a collective work
   - a part of a motion picture or other audiovisual work
   - a translation
   - a supplementary work
   - a compilation
   - an instructional text
   - a test
   - answer material for a test
   - an atlas

   if the parties expressly agree in a written instrument signed by them that the work shall be considered a work made for hire.

The authors of a joint work are co-owners of the copyright in the work, unless there is an agreement to the contrary.

Copyright in each separate contribution to a periodical or other collective work is distinct from copyright in the collective work as a whole and vests initially with the author of the contribution.

Two General Principles

- Mere ownership of a book, manuscript, painting, or any other copy or phonorecord does not give the possessor the copyright. The law provides that transfer of ownership of any material object that embodies a protected work does not of itself convey any rights in the copyright.

- Minors may claim copyright, but state laws may regulate the business dealings involving copyrights owned by minors. For information on relevant state laws, consult an attorney.

Copyright and National Origin of the Work

Copyright protection is available for all unpublished works, regardless of the nationality or domicile of the author.

Published works are eligible for copyright protection in the United States if *any* one of the following conditions is met:

- On the date of first publication, one or more of the authors is a national or domiciliary of the United States, or is a national, domiciliary, or sovereign authority of a treaty party,* or is a stateless person wherever that person may be domiciled; or

- The work is first published in the United States or in a foreign nation that, on the date of first publication, is a treaty party. For purposes of this condition, a work that is published in the United States or a treaty party within 30 days after publication in a foreign nation that is not a treaty party shall be considered to be first published in the United States or such treaty party, as the case may be; or

- The work is a sound recording that was first fixed in a treaty party; or

- The work is a pictorial, graphic, or sculptural work that is incorporated in a building or other structure, or an architectural work that is embodied in a building and the building or structure is located in the United States or a treaty party; or

- The work is first published by the United Nations or any of its specialized agencies, or by the Organization of American States; or

- The work is a foreign work that was in the public domain in the United States prior to 1996 and its copyright was restored under the Uruguay Round Agreements Act (URAA). Request Circular 38B, *Highlights of Copyright Amendments Contained in the Uruguay Round Agreements Act (URAA-GATT)*, for further information.

- The work comes within the scope of a Presidential proclamation.

*A treaty party is a country or intergovernmental organization other than the United States that is a party to an international agreement.

What Works Are Protected?

Copyright protects "original works of authorship" that are fixed in a tangible form of expression. The fixation need not be directly perceptible so long as it may be communicated with the aid of a machine or device. Copyrightable works include the following categories:

1 literary works

2 musical works, including any accompanying words

3 dramatic works, including any accompanying music

4 pantomimes and choreographic works

5 pictorial, graphic, and sculptural works

6 motion pictures and other audiovisual works

7 sound recordings

8 architectural works

These categories should be viewed broadly. For example, computer programs and most "compilations" may be registered as "literary works;" maps and architectural plans may be registered as "pictorial, graphic, and sculptural works."

What Is Not Protected by Copyright?

Several categories of material are generally not eligible for federal copyright protection. These include among others:

- Works that have *not* been fixed in a tangible form of expression (for example, choreographic works that have not been notated or recorded, or improvisational speeches or performances that have not been written or recorded)
- Titles, names, short phrases, and slogans; familiar symbols or designs; mere variations of typographic ornamentation, lettering, or coloring; mere listings of ingredients or contents
- Ideas, procedures, methods, systems, processes, concepts, principles, discoveries, or devices, as distinguished from a description, explanation, or illustration
- Works consisting *entirely* of information that is common property and containing no original authorship (for example: standard calendars, height and weight charts, tape measures and rulers, and lists or tables taken from public documents or other common sources)

How to Secure a Copyright

Copyright Secured Automatically upon Creation

The way in which copyright protection is secured is frequently misunderstood. No publication or registration or other action in the Copyright Office is required to secure copyright. (See following NOTE.) There are, however, certain definite advantages to registration. See "Copyright Registration" on page 7.

Copyright is secured *automatically* when the work is created, and a work is "created" when it is fixed in a copy or phonorecord for the first time. "Copies" are material objects from which a work can be read or visually perceived either directly or with the aid of a machine or device, such as books, manuscripts, sheet music, film, videotape, or microfilm. "Phonorecords" are material objects embodying fixations of sounds (excluding, by statutory definition, motion picture soundtracks), such as cassette tapes, CDs, or LPs. Thus, for example, a song (the "work") can be fixed in sheet music ("copies") or in phonograph disks ("phonorecords"), or both.

If a work is prepared over a period of time, the part of the work that is fixed on a particular date constitutes the created work as of that date.

Publication

Publication is no longer the key to obtaining federal copyright as it was under the Copyright Act of 1909. However, publication remains important to copyright owners.

The 1976 Copyright Act defines publication as follows:

"Publication" is the distribution of copies or phonorecords of a work to the public by sale or other transfer of ownership, or by rental, lease, or lending. The offering to distribute copies or phonorecords to a group of persons for purposes of further distribution, public performance, or public display constitutes publication. A public performance or display of a work does not of itself constitute publication.

NOTE: Before 1978, federal copyright was generally secured by the act of publication with notice of copyright, assuming compliance with all other relevant statutory conditions. U.S. works in the public domain on January 1, 1978, (for example, works published without satisfying all conditions for securing federal copyright under the Copyright Act of 1909) remain in the public domain under the 1976 Copyright Act.

Certain foreign works originally published without notice had their copyrights restored under the Uruguay Round Agreements Act (URAA). Request Circular 38B and see the "Notice of Copyright" section on page 4 of this publication for further information.

Federal copyright could also be secured before 1978 by the act of registration in the case of certain unpublished works and works eligible for ad interim copyright. The 1976 Copyright Act automatically extends to full term (section 304 sets the term) copyright for all works, including those subject to ad interim copyright if ad interim registration has been made on or before June 30, 1978.

A further discussion of the definition of "publication" can be found in the legislative history of the 1976 Copyright Act. The legislative reports define "to the public" as distribution to persons under no explicit or implicit restrictions with respect to disclosure of the contents. The reports state that the definition makes it clear that the sale of phonorecords constitutes publication of the underlying work, for example, the musical, dramatic, or literary work embodied in a phonorecord. The reports also state that it is clear that any form of dissemination in which the material object does not change hands, for example, performances or displays on television, is *not* a publication no matter how many people are exposed to the work. However, when copies or phonorecords are offered for sale or lease to a group of wholesalers, broadcasters, or motion picture theaters, publication does take place if the purpose is further distribution, public performance, or public display.

Publication is an important concept in the copyright law for several reasons:

- Works that are published in the United States are subject to mandatory deposit with the Library of Congress. See discussion on "Mandatory Deposit for Works Published in the United States" on page 9.

- Publication of a work can affect the limitations on the exclusive rights of the copyright owner that are set forth in sections 107 through 121 of the law.

- The year of publication may determine the duration of copyright protection for anonymous and pseudonymous works (when the author's identity is not revealed in the records of the Copyright Office) and for works made for hire.

- Deposit requirements for registration of published works differ from those for registration of unpublished works. See discussion on "Registration Procedures" on page 7.

- When a work is published, it may bear a notice of copyright to identify the year of publication and the name of the copyright owner and to inform the public that the work is protected by copyright. Copies of works published before March 1, 1989, *must* bear the notice or risk loss of copyright protection. See discussion on "Notice of Copyright" below.

Notice of Copyright

The use of a copyright notice is no longer required under U.S. law, although it is often beneficial. Because prior law did contain such a requirement, however, the use of notice is still relevant to the copyright status of older works.

Notice was required under the 1976 Copyright Act. This requirement was eliminated when the United States adhered to the Berne Convention, effective March 1, 1989. Although works published without notice before that date could have entered the public domain in the United States, the Uruguay Round Agreements Act (URAA) restores copyright in certain foreign works originally published without notice. For further information about copyright amendments in the URAA, request Circular 38B.

The Copyright Office does not take a position on whether copies of works first published with notice before March 1, 1989, which are distributed on or after March 1, 1989, must bear the copyright notice.

Use of the notice may be important because it informs the public that the work is protected by copyright, identifies the copyright owner, and shows the year of first publication. Furthermore, in the event that a work is infringed, if a proper notice of copyright appears on the published copy or copies to which a defendant in a copyright infringement suit had access, then no weight shall be given to such a defendant's interposition of a defense based on innocent infringement in mitigation of actual or statutory damages, except as provided in section 504(c)(2) of the copyright law. Innocent infringement occurs when the infringer did not realize that the work was protected.

The use of the copyright notice is the responsibility of the copyright owner and does not require advance permission from, or registration with, the Copyright Office.

Form of Notice for Visually Perceptible Copies

The notice for visually perceptible copies should contain all the following three elements:

1 **The symbol ©** (the letter C in a circle), or the word "Copyright," or the abbreviation "Copr."; and

2 **The year of first publication** of the work. In the case of compilations or derivative works incorporating previously published material, the year date of first publication of the compilation or derivative work is sufficient. The year date may be omitted where a pictorial, graphic, or sculptural work, with accompanying textual matter, if any, is reproduced in or on greeting cards, postcards, stationery, jewelry, dolls, toys, or any useful article; and

3 **The name of the owner of copyright** in the work, or an abbreviation by which the name can be recognized, or a generally known alternative designation of the owner.

Example: © 2004 *John Doe*

The "C in a circle" notice is used only on "visually perceptible copies." Certain kinds of works — for example, musical, dramatic, and literary works — may be fixed not in "copies" but by means of sound in an audio recording. Since audio recordings such as audio tapes and phonograph disks are "phonorecords" and not "copies," the "C in a circle" notice is not used to indicate protection of the underlying musical, dramatic, or literary work that is recorded.

Form of Notice for Phonorecords of Sound Recordings[1]

The notice for phonorecords embodying a sound recording should contain all the following three elements:

1 **The symbol** ℗ (the letter P in a circle); and

2 **The year of first publication** of the sound recording; and

3 **The name of the owner of copyright** in the sound recording, or an abbreviation by which the name can be recognized, or a generally known alternative designation of the owner. If the producer of the sound recording is named on the phonorecord label or container and if no other name appears in conjunction with the notice, the producer's name shall be considered a part of the notice.

> Example: ℗ *2004 A.B.C. Records Inc.*

NOTE: Since questions may arise from the use of variant forms of the notice, you may wish to seek legal advice before using any form of the notice other than those given here.

Position of Notice

The copyright notice should be affixed to copies or phonorecords in such a way as to "give reasonable notice of the claim of copyright." The three elements of the notice should ordinarily appear together on the copies or phonorecords or on the phonorecord label or container. The Copyright Office has issued regulations concerning the form and position of the copyright notice in the *Code of Federal Regulations* (37 CFR Section 201.20). For more information, request Circular 3, *Copyright Notice.*

Publications Incorporating U.S. Government Works

Works by the U.S. Government are not eligible for U.S. copyright protection. For works published on and after March 1, 1989, the previous notice requirement for works consisting primarily of one or more U.S. Government works has been eliminated. However, use of a notice on such a work will defeat a claim of innocent infringement as previously described provided the notice also includes a statement that identifies either those portions of the work in which copyright is claimed or those portions that constitute U.S. Government material.

> Example: © *2004 Jane Brown*
> *Copyright claimed in Chapters 7–10,*
> *exclusive of U. S. Government maps*

Copies of works published before March 1, 1989, that consist primarily of one or more works of the U.S. Government *should* have a notice and the identifying statement.

Unpublished Works

The author or copyright owner may wish to place a copyright notice on any unpublished copies or phonorecords that leave his or her control.

> Example: *Unpublished work* © *2004 Jane Doe*

Omission of Notice and Errors in Notice

The 1976 Copyright Act attempted to ameliorate the strict consequences of failure to include notice under prior law. It contained provisions that set out specific corrective steps to cure omissions or certain errors in notice. Under these provisions, an applicant had 5 years after publication to cure omission of notice or certain errors. Although these provisions are technically still in the law, their impact has been limited by the amendment making notice optional for all works published on and after March 1, 1989. For further information, request Circular 3.

How Long Copyright Protection Endures

Works Originally Created on or after January 1, 1978

A work that is created (fixed in tangible form for the first time) on or after January 1, 1978, is automatically protected from the moment of its creation and is ordinarily given a term enduring for the author's life plus an additional 70 years after the author's death. In the case of "a joint work prepared by two or more authors who did not work for hire," the term lasts for 70 years after the last surviving author's death. For works made for hire, and for anonymous and pseudonymous works (unless the author's identity is revealed in Copyright Office records), the duration of copyright will be 95 years from publication or 120 years from creation, whichever is shorter.

Works Originally Created Before January 1, 1978, But Not Published or Registered by That Date

These works have been automatically brought under the statute and are now given federal copyright protection. The duration of copyright in these works will generally be computed in the same way as for works created on or after January 1, 1978: the life-plus-70 or 95/120-year terms will apply to them as well. The law provides that in no case will the term of copyright for works in this category expire before December 31, 2002, and for works published on or before December 31, 2002, the term of copyright will not expire before December 31, 2047.

Works Originally Created and Published or Registered before January 1, 1978

Under the law in effect before 1978, copyright was secured either on the date a work was published with a copyright notice or on the date of registration if the work was registered in unpublished form. In either case, the copyright endured for a first term of 28 years from the date it was secured. During the last (28th) year of the first term, the copyright was eligible for renewal. The Copyright Act of 1976 extended the renewal term from 28 to 47 years for copyrights that were subsisting on January 1, 1978, or for pre-1978 copyrights restored under the Uruguay Round Agreements Act (URAA), making these works eligible for a total term of protection of 75 years. Public Law 105-298, enacted on October 27, 1998, further extended the renewal term of copyrights still subsisting on that date by an additional 20 years, providing for a renewal term of 67 years and a total term of protection of 95 years.

Public Law 102-307, enacted on June 26, 1992, amended the 1976 Copyright Act to provide for automatic renewal of the term of copyrights secured between January 1, 1964, and December 31, 1977. Although the renewal term is automatically provided, the Copyright Office does not issue a renewal certificate for these works unless a renewal application and fee are received and registered in the Copyright Office.

Public Law 102-307 makes renewal registration optional. Thus, filing for renewal registration is no longer required in order to extend the original 28-year copyright term to the full 95 years. However, some benefits accrue from making a renewal registration during the 28th year of the original term.

For more detailed information on renewal of copyright and the copyright term, request Circular 15, *Renewal of Copyright*; Circular 15A, *Duration of Copyright*; and Circular 15T, *Extension of Copyright Terms*.

Transfer of Copyright

Any or all of the copyright owner's exclusive rights or any subdivision of those rights may be transferred, but the transfer of *exclusive* rights is not valid unless that transfer is in writing and signed by the owner of the rights conveyed or such owner's duly authorized agent. Transfer of a right on a nonexclusive basis does not require a written agreement.

A copyright may also be conveyed by operation of law and may be bequeathed by will or pass as personal property by the applicable laws of intestate succession.

Copyright is a personal property right, and it is subject to the various state laws and regulations that govern the ownership, inheritance, or transfer of personal property as well as terms of contracts or conduct of business. For information about relevant state laws, consult an attorney.

Transfers of copyright are normally made by contract. The Copyright Office does not have any forms for such transfers. The law does provide for the recordation in the Copyright Office of transfers of copyright ownership. Although recordation is not required to make a valid transfer between the parties, it does provide certain legal advantages and may be required to validate the transfer as against third parties. For information on recordation of transfers and other documents related to copyright, request Circular 12, *Recordation of Transfers and Other Documents*.

Termination of Transfers

Under the previous law, the copyright in a work reverted to the author, if living, or if the author was not living, to other specified beneficiaries, provided a renewal claim was registered in the 28th year of the original term.* The present law drops the renewal feature except for works already in the first term of statutory protection when the present law took effect. Instead, the present law permits termination of a grant of rights after 35 years under certain conditions by serving written notice on the transferee within specified time limits.

For works already under statutory copyright protection before 1978, the present law provides a similar right of termination covering the newly added years that extended the former maximum term of the copyright from 56 to 95 years. For further information, request Circulars 15A and 15T.

*The copyright in works eligible for renewal on or after June 26, 1992, will vest in the name of the renewal claimant on the effective date of any renewal registration made during the 28th year of the original term. Otherwise, the renewal copyright will vest in the party entitled to claim renewal as of December 31st of the 28th year.

International Copyright Protection

There is no such thing as an "international copyright" that will automatically protect an author's writings throughout the entire world. Protection against unauthorized use in a particular country depends, basically, on the national laws of that country. However, most countries do offer protection to foreign works under certain conditions, and these conditions have been greatly simplified by international copyright treaties and conventions. For further information and a list of countries that maintain copyright relations with the United States, request Circular 38A, *International Copyright Relations of the United States*.

Copyright Registration

In general, copyright registration is a legal formality intended to make a public record of the basic facts of a particular copyright. However, registration is not a condition of copyright protection. Even though registration is not a requirement for protection, the copyright law provides several inducements or advantages to encourage copyright owners to make registration. Among these advantages are the following:

- Registration establishes a public record of the copyright claim.

- Before an infringement suit may be filed in court, registration is necessary for works of U.S. origin.

- If made before or within 5 years of publication, registration will establish *prima facie* evidence in court of the validity of the copyright and of the facts stated in the certificate.

- If registration is made within 3 months after publication of the work or prior to an infringement of the work, statutory damages and attorney's fees will be available to the copyright owner in court actions. Otherwise, only an award of actual damages and profits is available to the copyright owner.

- Registration allows the owner of the copyright to record the registration with the U.S. Customs Service for protection against the importation of infringing copies. For additional information, request Publication No. 563, *How to Protect Your Intellectual Property Right*, from: U.S. Customs Service, P.O. Box 7404, Washington, D.C. 20044. See the U.S. Customs Service website at *www.customs.gov* for online publications.

Registration may be made at any time within the life of the copyright. Unlike the law before 1978, when a work has been registered in unpublished form, it is not necessary to make another registration when the work becomes published, although the copyright owner may register the published edition, if desired.

Registration Procedures

Original Registration

To register a work, send the following three elements in the same envelope or package to:

Library of Congress
Copyright Office
101 Independence Avenue, S.E.
Washington, D.C. 20559-6000

1 A properly completed application form.

2 A nonrefundable filing fee of $30 for each application.

3 A nonreturnable deposit of the work being registered. The deposit requirements vary in particular situations. The *general* requirements follow. Also note the information under "Special Deposit Requirements" on page 8.

- If the work is unpublished, one complete copy or phonorecord.

- If the work was first published in the United States on or after January 1, 1978, two complete copies or phonorecords of the best edition.

- If the work was first published in the United States before January 1, 1978, two complete copies or phonorecords of the work as first published.

- If the work was first published outside the United States, one complete copy or phonorecord of the work as first published.

- If sending multiple works, all applications, deposits, and fees should be sent in the same package. If possible, applications should be attached to the appropriate deposit. Whenever possible, number each package (*e.g.*, 1 of 3, 2 of 4) to facilitate processing.

NOTE: For current information on fees, please write the Copyright Office, check the Copyright Office website at *www.copyright.gov*, or call (202) 707-3000.

What Happens if the Three Elements Are Not Received Together

Applications and fees received without appropriate copies, phonorecords, or identifying material will *not* be processed and ordinarily will be returned. Unpublished deposits without applications or fees ordinarily will be returned, also. In most cases, published deposits received without applications and fees can be immediately transferred to the collections of the Library of Congress. This practice is in accordance with section 408 of the law, which provides that the published deposit required for the collections of the Library of Congress may be used for registration only if the deposit is "accompanied by the prescribed application and fee…."

After the deposit is received and transferred to another service unit of the Library for its collections or other disposition, it is no longer available to the Copyright Office. If you wish to register the work, you must deposit additional copies or phonorecords with your application and fee.

Renewal Registration

To register a renewal, send:

1 A properly completed application Form RE and, if necessary, Form RE Addendum, *and*

2 A nonrefundable filing fee of $60 without Addendum; $90 with Addendum for each application. Copyright Office fees are subject to change. For current fees, please check the Copyright Office website at *www.copyright.gov*, write the Copyright Office, or call (202) 707-3000. Each Addendum form must be accompanied by a deposit representing the work being renewed. See Circular 15, *Renewal of Copyright.*

NOTE: *Complete the application form using black ink pen or type.* You may photocopy blank application forms. However, photocopied forms submitted to the Copyright Office must be clear, legible, on a good grade of 8½-inch by 11-inch white paper suitable for automatic feeding through a photocopier. The forms should be printed, preferably in black ink, head-to-head so that when you turn the sheet over, the top of page 2 is directly behind the top of page 1. *Forms not meeting these requirements may be returned resulting in delayed registration.*

Special Deposit Requirements

Special deposit requirements exist for many types of works. The following are prominent examples of exceptions to the general deposit requirements:

• If the work is a motion picture, the deposit requirement is one complete copy of the unpublished or published motion picture *and* a separate written description of its contents, such as a continuity, press book, or synopsis.

• If the work is a literary, dramatic, or musical work *published only in a phonorecord*, the deposit requirement is one complete phonorecord.

• If the work is an unpublished or published computer program, the deposit requirement is one visually perceptible copy in source code of the *first 25 and last 25 pages* of the program. For a program of fewer than 50 pages, the deposit is a copy of the entire program. For more information on computer program registration, including deposits for revised programs and provisions for trade secrets, request Circular 61, *Copyright Registration for Computer Programs.*

• If the work is in a CD-ROM format, the deposit requirement is one complete copy of the material, that is, the CD-ROM, the operating software, and any manual(s) accompanying it. If registration is sought for the computer program on the CD-ROM, the deposit should also include a printout of the first 25 and last 25 pages of source code for the program.

In the case of works reproduced in three-dimensional copies, identifying material such as photographs or drawings is ordinarily required. Other examples of special deposit requirements (but by no means an exhaustive list) include many works of the visual arts such as greeting cards, toys, fabrics, and oversized materials (request Circular 40A, *Deposit Requirements for Registration of Claims to Copyright in Visual Arts Material*); video games and other machine-readable audiovisual works (request Circular 61); automated databases (request Circular 65, *Copyright Registration for Automated Databases*); and contributions to collective works. For information about deposit requirements for group registration of serials, request Circular 62, *Copyright Registration for Serials.*

If you are unsure of the deposit requirement for your work, write or call the Copyright Office and describe the work you wish to register.

Unpublished Collections

Under the following conditions, a work may be registered in unpublished form as a "collection," with one application form and one fee:

• The elements of the collection are assembled in an orderly form;

• The combined elements bear a single title identifying the collection as a whole;

• The copyright claimant in all the elements and in the collection as a whole is the same; and

• All the elements are by the same author, or, if they are by different authors, at least one of the authors has contributed copyrightable authorship to each element.

NOTE: A *Library of Congress Control Number* is different from a copyright registration number. The Cataloging in Publication (CIP) Division of the Library of Congress is responsible for assigning LC Control Numbers and is operationally separate from the Copyright Office. A book may be registered in or deposited with the Copyright Office but not necessarily cataloged and added to the Library's collections. For information about obtaining an LC Control Number, see the following website: *http://pcn.loc.gov/pcn.* For information on International Standard Book Numbering (ISBN), write to: ISBN, R.R. Bowker, 630 Central Ave., New Providence, NJ 07974. Call (877) 310-7333. For further information and to apply online, see *www.isbn.org.* For information on International Standard Serial Numbering (ISSN), write to: Library of Congress, National Serials Data Program, Serial Record Division, Washington, D.C. 20540-4160. Call (202) 707-6452. Or obtain information from *www.loc.gov/issn.*

An unpublished collection is not indexed under the individual titles of the contents but under the title of the collection.

Effective Date of Registration

A copyright registration is effective on the date the Copyright Office receives all the required elements in acceptable form, regardless of how long it then takes to process the application and mail the certificate of registration. The time the Copyright Office requires to process an application varies, depending on the amount of material the Office is receiving.

If you apply for copyright registration, you will not receive an acknowledgment that your application has been received (the Office receives more than 600,000 applications annually), but you can expect:

· A letter or a telephone call from a Copyright Office staff member if further information is needed or

· A certificate of registration indicating that the work has been registered, or if the application cannot be accepted, a letter explaining why it has been rejected.

Requests to have certificates available for pickup in the Public Information Office or to have certificates sent by Federal Express or another mail service cannot be honored.

If you want to know the date that the Copyright Office receives your material, send it by registered or certified mail and request a return receipt.

Corrections and Amplifications of Existing Registrations

To correct an error in a copyright registration or to amplify the information given in a registration, file a supplementary registration form—Form CA—with the Copyright Office. The filing fee is $100. (See note on page 7.) The information in a supplementary registration augments but does not supersede that contained in the earlier registration. Note also that a supplementary registration is not a substitute for an original registration, for a renewal registration, or for recording a transfer of ownership. For further information about supplementary registration, request Circular 8, *Supplementary Copyright Registration*.

Mandatory Deposit for Works Published in the United States

Although a copyright registration is not required, the Copyright Act establishes a mandatory deposit requirement for works published in the United States. See the definition of "publication" on page 3. In general, the owner of copyright or the owner of the exclusive right of publication in the work has a legal obligation to deposit in the Copyright Office, within 3 months of publication in the United States, two copies (or in the case of sound recordings, two phonorecords) for the use of the Library of Congress. Failure to make the deposit can result in fines and other penalties but does not affect copyright protection.

Certain categories of works are *exempt entirely* from the mandatory deposit requirements, and the obligation is reduced for certain other categories. For further information about mandatory deposit, request Circular 7D, *Mandatory Deposit of Copies or Phonorecords for the Library of Congress*.

Use of Mandatory Deposit to Satisfy Registration Requirements

For works published in the United States, the copyright law contains a provision under which a single deposit can be made to satisfy both the deposit requirements for the Library and the registration requirements. In order to have this dual effect, the copies or phonorecords must be accompanied by the prescribed application form and filing fee.

Who May File an Application Form?

The following persons are legally entitled to submit an application form:

· **The author.** This is either the person who actually created the work or, if the work was made for hire, the employer or other person for whom the work was prepared.

· **The copyright claimant.** The copyright claimant is defined in Copyright Office regulations as either the author of the work or a person or organization that has obtained ownership of all the rights under the copyright initially belonging to the author. This category includes a person or organization who has obtained by contract the right to claim legal title to the copyright in an application for copyright registration.

· **The owner of exclusive right(s).** Under the law, any of the exclusive rights that make up a copyright and any subdivision of them can be transferred and owned separately, even though the transfer may be limited in time or place of effect. The term "copyright owner" with respect to any one of the exclusive rights contained in a copyright refers to the owner of that particular right. Any owner of an exclusive right may apply for registration of a claim in the work.

- **The duly authorized agent of such author,** other copyright claimant, or owner of exclusive right(s). Any person authorized to act on behalf of the author, other copyright claimant, or owner of exclusive rights may apply for registration.

There is no requirement that applications be prepared or filed by an attorney.

Application Forms

For Original Registration

- **Form PA:** for published and unpublished works of the performing arts (musical and dramatic works, pantomimes and choreographic works, motion pictures and other audiovisual works)
- **Form SE:** for serials, works issued or intended to be issued in successive parts bearing numerical or chronological designations and intended to be continued indefinitely (periodicals, newspapers, magazines, newsletters, annuals, journals, etc.)
- **Form SR:** for published and unpublished sound recordings
- **Form TX:** for published and unpublished nondramatic literary works
- **Form VA:** for published and unpublished works of the visual arts (pictorial, graphic, and sculptural works, including architectural works)
- **Form G/DN:** a specialized form to register a complete month's issues of a daily newspaper and newsletter when certain conditions are met
- **Short Form/SE and Form SE/Group:** specialized SE forms for use when certain requirements are met
- **Short Forms TX, PA, and VA:** short versions of applications for original registration. For further information about using the short forms, request publication SL-7.
- **Form GATT and Form GATT/GRP:** specialized forms to register a claim in a work or group of related works in which U.S. copyright was restored under the 1994 Uruguay Round Agreements Act (URAA). For further information, request Circular 38B.

For Renewal Registration

- **Form RE:** for claims to renew copyright in works copyrighted under the law in effect through December 31, 1977 (1909 Copyright Act) and registered during the initial 28-year copyright term
- **Form RE Addendum:** accompanies Form RE for claims to renew copyright in works copyrighted under the 1909 Copyright Act but never registered during their initial 28-year copyright term

For Corrections and Amplifications

- **Form CA:** for supplementary registration to correct or amplify information given in the Copyright Office record of an earlier registration

For a Group of Contributions to Periodicals

- **Form GR/CP:** an adjunct application to be used for registration of a group of contributions to periodicals in addition to an application Form TX, PA, or VA

How to Obtain Application Forms

See "For Further Information" on page 11.

You must have Adobe Acrobat Reader® installed on your computer to view and print the forms accessed on the Internet. Adobe Acrobat Reader may be downloaded free from Adobe Systems Incorporated through links from the same Internet site from which the forms are available.

Print forms head to head (top of page 2 is directly behind the top of page 1) on a single piece of good quality, 8½-inch by 11-inch white paper. To achieve the best quality copies of the application forms, use a laser printer.

Fill-In Forms Available

All Copyright Office forms are available on the Copyright Office Website in fill-in version. Go to *www.copyright.gov* and follow the instructions. The fill-in forms allow you to enter information while the form is displayed on the screen by an Adobe Acrobat Reader product. You may then print the completed form and mail it to the Copyright Office. Fill-in forms provide a clean, sharp printout for your records and for filing with the Copyright Office.

Fees

All remittances should be in the form of drafts, that is, checks, money orders, or bank drafts, payable to *Register of Copyrights*. Do not send cash. Drafts must be redeemable without service or exchange fee through a U.S. institution, must be payable in U.S. dollars, and must be imprinted with American Banking Association routing numbers. International Money Orders and Postal Money Orders that are negotiable only at a post office are not acceptable.

If a check received in payment of the filing fee is returned to the Copyright Office as uncollectible, the Copyright Office will cancel the registration and will notify the remitter.

The filing fee for processing an original, supplementary, or renewal claim is nonrefundable, whether or not copyright registration is ultimately made.

Do not send cash. The Copyright Office cannot assume any responsibility for the loss of currency sent in payment of copyright fees. For further information, request Circular 4, *Copyright Fees.*

*NOTE: Copyright Office fees are subject to change. For current fees, please check the Copyright Office website at *www.copyright.gov*, write the Copyright Office, or call (202) 707 3000.

Certain Fees and Services May Be Charged to a Credit Card

Some fees may be charged by telephone and in person in the office. Others may only be charged in person in the office. Credit card payments are generally authorized only for services that do not require filing of applications or other materials. An exception is made for fees related to items that are hand-carried into the Public Information Office.

- **Certifications and Documents Section:** These fees may be charged in person in the office or by phone: additional certificates; copies of documents and deposits; searching, locating and retrieving deposits; certifications; and expedited processing.

- **Public Information Office:** These fees may only be charged in person in the office, not by phone: standard registration request forms; special handling requests for all standard registration requests; requests for services provided by the Certifications and Documents Section when the request is accompanied by a request for special handling; search requests for which a fee estimate has been provided; additional fee for each claim using the same deposit; full term retention fees; appeal fees; Secure Test processing fee; short fee payments when accompanied by a Remittance Due Notice; in-process retrieval fees; and online service providers fees.

- **Reference and Bibliography Section:** Requests for searches on a regular or expedited basis can be charged to a credit card by phone.

- **Records Maintenance Unit:** Computer time on COINS, printing from the Optical Disk, and photocopying can be charged in person in the office.

- **Fiscal Control Section:** Deposit Accounts maintained by the Fiscal Control Section may be replenished by credit card. See Circular 5, *How to Open and Maintain a Deposit Account in the Copyright Office.*

NIE recordations and claims filed on Forms GATT and GATT/GRP may be paid by credit card if the card number is included in a separate letter that accompanies the form.

Search of Copyright Office Records

The records of the Copyright Office are open for inspection and searching by the public. Moreover, on request, the Copyright Office will search its records for you at the statutory hourly rate of $75 for each hour or fraction of an hour. (See note above.) For information on searching the Office records concerning the copyright status or ownership of a work, request Circular 22, *How to Investigate the Copyright Status of a Work*, and Circular 23, *The Copyright Card Catalog and the Online Files of the Copyright Office.*

Copyright Office records in machine-readable form cataloged from January 1, 1978, to the present, including registration and renewal information and recorded documents, are now available for searching on the Internet via the Copyright Office website at *www.copyright.gov.*

For Further Information

Information via the Internet

Frequently requested circulars, announcements, regulations, other related materials, and all copyright application forms are available via the Internet. You may access these from the Copyright Office website at *www.copyright.gov.*

Information by fax

Circulars and other information (but not application forms) are available by using a touchtone phone to access Fax-on-Demand at (202) 707-2600.

Information by telephone

For general information about copyright, call the Copyright Public Information Office at (202) 707-3000. The TTY number is (202) 707-6737. Information specialists are on duty from 8:30 a.m. to 5:00 p.m., eastern time, Monday through Friday, except federal holidays. Recorded information is available 24 hours a day. Or, if you know which application forms and circulars you want, request them 24 hours a day from the Forms and Publications Hotline at (202) 707-9100. Leave a recorded message.

Information by regular mail

Write to:

> Library of Congress
> Copyright Office
> Publications Section, LM-455
> 101 Independence Avenue, S.E.
> Washington, D.C. 20559-6000

For a list of other material published by the Copyright Office, request Circular 2, *Publications on Copyright*.

The Copyright Public Information Office is open to the public 8:30 a.m. to 5:00 p.m. Monday through Friday, eastern time, except federal holidays. The office is located in the Library of Congress, James Madison Memorial Building, Room 401, at 101 Independence Avenue, S.E., Washington, D.C., near the Capitol South Metro stop. Information specialists are available to answer questions, provide circulars, and accept applications for registration. Access for disabled individuals is at the front door on Independence Avenue, S.E.

The Copyright Office is not permitted to give legal advice. If information or guidance is needed on matters such as disputes over the ownership of a copyright, suits against possible infringers, the procedure for getting a work published, or the method of obtaining royalty payments, it may be necessary to consult an attorney.

NOTE: The Copyright Office provides a free electronic mailing list, *NewsNet*, that issues periodic email messages on the subject of copyright. The messages alert subscribers to hearings, deadlines for comments, new and proposed regulations, new publications, and other copyright-related subjects of interest. *NewsNet* is not an interactive discussion group. To subscribe, send a message to *listserv@loc.gov*. In the body of the message say "subscribe uscopyright". Or fill in the subscription form online at *www.copyright.gov/newsnet*. You will receive a standard welcoming message indicating that your subscription to *NewsNet* has been accepted.

Endnote

1. Sound recordings are defined in the law as "works that result from the fixation of a series of musical, spoken, or other sounds, but not including the sounds accompanying a motion picture or other audiovisual work." Common examples include recordings of music, drama, or lectures. A sound recording is not the same as a phonorecord. A phonorecord is the physical object in which works of authorship are embodied. The word "phonorecord" includes cassette tapes, CDs, LPs, 45 r.p.m. disks, as well as other formats.

U.S. Copyright Office · The Library of Congress · 101 Independence Avenue, SE · Washington, DC 20559-6000 · www.copyright.gov

CIRCULAR 1   PRINT REV: 01/2004—30,000   WEB REV: 01/2004   Printed on recycled paper   U.S. GOVERNMENT PRINTING OFFICE: 2004-304-447/60.045

©opyright
United States Copyright Office

How to Investigate the Copyright Status of a Work

In General

Methods of Approaching a Copyright Investigation

There are several ways to investigate whether a work is under copyright protection and, if so, the facts of the copyright. These are the main ones:

1 Examine a copy of the work for such elements as a copyright notice, place and date of publication, author and publisher. If the work is a sound recording, examine the disk, tape cartridge, or cassette in which the recorded sound is fixed, or the album cover, sleeve, or container in which the recording is sold.

2 Make a search of the Copyright Office catalogs and other records, *or*

3 Have the Copyright Office make a search for you.

A Few Words of Caution About Copyright Investigations

Copyright investigations often involve more than one of these methods. Even if you follow all three approaches, the results may not be conclusive. Moreover, as explained in this circular, the changes brought about under the Copyright Act of 1976, the Berne Convention Implementation Act of 1988, the Copyright Renewal Act of 1992, and the Sonny Bono Copyright Term Extension Act of 1998 must be considered when investigating the copyright status of a work.

This circular offers some practical guidance on what to look for if you are making a copyright investigation. It is important to realize, however, that this circular contains only general information and that there are a number of exceptions to the principles outlined here. In many cases it is important to consult with a copyright attorney before reaching any conclusions regarding the copyright status of a work.

How to Search Copyright Office Catalogs and Records

Catalog of Copyright Entries

The Copyright Office published the *Catalog of Copyright Entries* (CCE) in printed format from 1891 through 1978. From 1979 through 1982 the CCE was issued in microfiche format. The catalog was divided into parts according to the classes of works registered. Each CCE segment covered all registrations made during a particular period of time. Renewal registrations made from 1979 through 1982 are found in Section 8 of the catalog. Renewals prior to that time were generally listed at the end of the volume containing the class of work to which they pertained.

A number of libraries throughout the United States maintain copies of the *Catalog*, and this may provide a good starting point if you wish to make a search yourself. There are some cases, however, in which a search of the *Catalog* alone will not be sufficient to provide the needed information. For example:

- Because the *Catalog* does not include entries for assignments or other recorded documents, it cannot be used for searches involving the ownership of rights.

- The *Catalog* entry contains the essential facts concerning a registration, but it is not a verbatim transcript of the registration record. It does not contain the address of the copyright claimant.

Effective with registrations made since 1982 when the CCE was discontinued, the only method of searching outside the Library of Congress is by using the Internet to access the automated catalog. The automated catalog contains entries from 1978 to the present. Information for accessing the catalog via the Internet is provided below.

Individual Searches of Copyright Records

The Copyright Office is located in the Library of Congress James Madison Memorial Building, 101 Independence Avenue, S.E., Washington, D.C. 20559-6000.

Most Copyright Office records are open to public inspection and searching from 8:30 a.m. to 5 p.m., eastern time, Monday through Friday, except federal holidays. The various records freely available to the public include an extensive card catalog, an automated catalog containing records from 1978 forward, record books, and microfilm records of assignments and related documents. Other records, including correspondence files and deposit copies, are not open to the public for searching. However, they may be inspected upon request and payment of a $75 per hour search fee.*

*NOTE: Copyright Office fees are subject to change. For current fees, please check the Copyright Office website at www.copyright.gov, write the Copyright Office, or call (202) 707 3000.

If you wish to do your own searching in the Copyright Office files open to the public, you will be given assistance in locating the records you need and in learning procedures for searching. If the Copyright Office staff actually makes the search for you, a search fee must be charged. The search will not be done while you wait.

In addition, the following files dating from 1978 forward are now available from the Copyright Office website at *www.copyright.gov*: COHM, which includes all material except serials and documents; COHD, which includes documents; and COHS, which includes serials.

The Copyright Office does not offer search assistance to users on the Internet.

Searching by the Copyright Office

In General

Upon request, the Copyright Office staff will search its records at the statutory rate of $75* for each hour or fraction of an hour consumed. Based on the information you furnish, we will provide an estimate of the total search fee. If you decide to have the Office staff conduct the search, you should send the estimated amount with your request. The Office will then proceed with the search and send you a typewritten report or, if you prefer, an oral report by telephone. If you request an oral report, please provide a telephone number where you can be reached from 8:30 a.m. to 5 p.m., eastern time.

Search reports can be certified on request for an extra fee of $80 per hour.* Certified searches are most frequently requested to meet the evidentiary requirements of litigation.

Your request and any other correspondence should be addressed to:

Library of Congress
Copyright Office
Reference and Bibliography Section, LM-451
101 Independence Avenue, S.E.
Washington, D.C. 20559-6000
PHONE: (202) 707-6850
FAX: (202) 252-3485
TTY: (202) 707-6737

What the Fee Does Not Cover

The search fee does *not* include the cost of additional certificates, photocopies of deposits, or copies of other Office records. For information concerning these services, request Circular 6, *Obtaining Access to and Copies of Copyright Office Records and Deposits.*

Information Needed

The more detailed information you can furnish with your request, the less expensive the search will be. Please provide as much of the following information as possible:

- The title of the work, with any possible variants
- The names of the authors, including possible pseudonyms
- The name of the probable copyright owner, which may be the publisher or producer
- The approximate year when the work was published or registered
- The type of work involved (book, play, musical composition, sound recording, photograph, etc.)
- For a work originally published as a part of a periodical or collection, the title of that publication and any other information, such as the volume or issue number, to help identify it
- The registration number or any other copyright data

Motion pictures are often based on other works such as books or serialized contributions to periodicals or other composite works. *If you desire a search for an underlying work or for music from a motion picture, you must specifically request such a search. You must also identify the underlying works and music and furnish the specific titles, authors, and approximate dates of these works.*

Searches Involving Assignments and Other Documents Affecting Copyright Ownership

For the standard hourly search fee, the Copyright Office staff will search its indexes covering the records of assignments and other recorded documents concerning ownership of copyrights. The reports of searches in these cases will state the facts shown in the Office's indexes of the recorded documents but will offer no interpretation of the content of the documents or their legal effect.

Limitations on Searches

In determining whether or not to have a search made, you should keep the following points in mind:

No Special Lists · The Copyright Office does not maintain any listings of works by subject or any lists of works that are in the public domain.

Contributions Not Listed Separately in Copyright Office Records · Individual works such as stories, poems, articles, or musical compositions that were published as contributions to a copyrighted periodical or collection are usually not listed separately by title in our records.

No Comparisons · The Copyright Office does not search or compare copies of works to determine questions of possible infringement or to determine how much two or more versions of a work have in common.

Titles and Names Not Copyrightable · Copyright does not protect names and titles, and our records list many different works identified by the same or similar titles. Some brand names, trade names, slogans, and phrases may be entitled to protection under the general rules of law relating to unfair competition. They may also be entitled to registration under the provisions of the trademark laws. Questions about the trademark laws should be addressed to the Commissioner of Patents and Trademarks, Washington, D.C. 20231. Possible protection of names and titles under common law principles of unfair competition is a question of state law.

No Legal Advice · The Copyright Office cannot express any opinion as to the legal significance or effect of the facts included in a search report.

Some Words of Caution

Searches Not Always Conclusive

Searches of the Copyright Office catalogs and records are useful in helping to determine the copyright status of a work, but they cannot be regarded as conclusive in all cases. The complete absence of any information about a work in the Office records does not mean that the work is unprotected. The following are examples of cases in which information about a particular work may be incomplete or lacking entirely in the Copyright Office:

- Before 1978, unpublished works were entitled to protection under common law without the need of registration.
- Works published with notice prior to 1978 may be registered at *any* time within the first 28-year term.
- Works copyrighted between January 1, 1964, and December 31, 1977, are affected by the Copyright Renewal Act of 1992, which automatically extends the copyright term and makes renewal registrations optional.
- For works under copyright protection on or after January 1, 1978, registration may be made at any time during the term of protection. Although registration is not required as a condition of copyright protection, there are certain definite advantages to registration. For further information, request Circular 1, *Copyright Basics*.
- Since searches are ordinarily limited to registrations that have already been cataloged, a search report may not cover recent registrations for which catalog records are not yet available.

- The information in the search request may not have been complete or specific enough to identify the work.
- The work may have been registered under a different title or as part of a larger work.

Protection in Foreign Countries

Even if you conclude that a work is in the public domain in the United States, this does not necessarily mean that you are free to use it in other countries. Every nation has its own laws governing the length and scope of copyright protection, and these are applicable to uses of the work within that nation's borders. Thus, the expiration or loss of copyright protection in the United States may still leave the work fully protected against unauthorized use in other countries.

Other Circulars

For further information, request Circular 6, *Obtaining Access to and Copies of Copyright Office Records and Deposits*; Circular 15, *Renewal of Copyright*; Circular 15A, *Duration of Copyright*; and Circular 15T, *Extension of Copyright Terms*, from:

Library of Congress
Copyright Office
Publications Section, LM-455
101 Independence Avenue, S.E.
Washington, D.C. 20559-6000

You may call the Forms and Publications Hotline (202) 707-9100 at any time, day or night, to leave a recorded request for forms or circulars. Requests are filled and mailed promptly.

Impact of the Copyright Act on Copyright Investigations

On October 19, 1976, the President signed into law a complete revision of the copyright law of the United States (title 17 of the *United States Code*). Most provisions of this statute came into force on January 1, 1978, superseding the copyright act of 1909. These provisions made significant changes in the copyright law. Further important changes resulted from the Berne Convention Implementation Act of 1988, which took effect March 1, 1989; the Copyright Renewal Act of 1992 (P.L. 102-307) enacted June 26, 1992, which amended the renewal provisions of the copyright law; and the Sonny Bono Copyright Term Extension Act of 1998 (P.L. 105-298) enacted October 27, 1998, which extended the term of copyrights for an additional 20 years.

If you need more information about the provisions of either the 1909 or the 1976 law, write or call the Copyright Office. For information about renewals, request Circular 15, *Renewal of Copyright*. For information about the Sonny Bono Copyright Term Extension Act, request SL-15, *New Terms for Copyright Protection*. For copies of the law ($24.00 each), request Circular 92, *Copyright Law of the United States*, (stock number is changed to 030-002-00197-7) from:

Superintendent of Documents
P.O. Box 371954
Pittsburgh, PA 15250-7954
PHONE: (202) 512-1800 [toll free: (866) 512-1800]
FAX: (202) 512-2250

For copyright investigations, the following points about the impact of the Copyright Act of 1976, the Berne Convention Implementation Act of 1988, and the Copyright Renewal Act of 1992 should be considered.

A Changed System of Copyright Formalities

Some of the most sweeping changes under the 1976 Copyright Act involve copyright formalities, that is, the procedural requirements for securing and maintaining full copyright protection. The old system of formalities involved copyright notice, deposit and registration, recordation of transfers and licenses of copyright ownership, and United States manufacture, among other things. In general, while retaining formalities, the 1976 law reduced the chances of mistakes, softened the consequences of errors and omissions, and allowed for the correction of errors.

The Berne Convention Implementation Act of 1988 reduced formalities, most notably making the addition of the previously mandatory copyright notice optional. It should be noted that the amended notice requirements are not retroactive.

The Copyright Renewal Act of 1992, enacted June 26, 1992, automatically extends the term of copyrights secured between January 1, 1964, and December 31, 1977, making renewal registration optional. Consult Circular 15, *Renewal of Copyright*, for details. For additional information, you may contact the Renewals Section.

PHONE: (202) 707-8180
FAX: (202) 707-3849

Automatic Copyright

Under the present copyright law, copyright exists in original works of authorship created and fixed in any tangible medium of expression, now known or later developed, from which they can be perceived, reproduced, or otherwise communicated, either directly, or indirectly with the aid of a machine or device. In other words, copyright is an incident of creative authorship not dependent on statutory formalities. Thus, registration with the Copyright Office generally is not required, but there are certain advantages that arise from a timely registration. For further information on the advantages of registration, write or call the Copyright Office and request Circular 1, *Copyright Basics.*

Copyright Notice

The 1909 Copyright Act and the 1976 Copyright Act as originally enacted required a notice of copyright on published works. For most works, a copyright notice consisted of the symbol ©, the word "Copyright" or the abbreviation "Copr.," together with the name of the owner of copyright and the year of first publication. For example: "© Joan Crane 2004" or "Copyright 2004 by Abraham Adams."

For sound recordings published on or after February 15, 1972, a copyright notice might read "℗ 1994 XYZ Records, Inc." See below for more information about sound recordings.

For mask works, a copyright notice might read "Ⓜ SDR Industries." Request Circular 100, *Federal Statutory Protection for Mask Works,* for more information.

As originally enacted, the 1976 law prescribed that all visually perceptible published copies of a work, or published phonorecords of a sound recording, should bear a proper copyright notice. This applies to such works published before March 1, 1989. After March 1, 1989, notice of copyright on these works is optional. Adding the notice, however, is strongly encouraged and, if litigation involving the copyright occurs, certain advantages exist for publishing a work with notice.

Prior to March 1, 1989, the requirement for the notice applied equally whether the work was published in the United States or elsewhere by authority of the copyright owner. Compliance with the statutory notice requirements was the responsibility of the copyright owner. Unauthorized publication without the copyright notice, or with a defective notice, does not affect the validity of the copyright in the work.

Advance permission from, or registration with, the Copyright Office is not required before placing a copyright notice on copies of the work or on phonorecords of a sound recording. Moreover, for works first published on or after January 1, 1978, through February 28, 1989, omission of the required notice, or use of a defective notice, did not result in forfeiture or outright loss of copyright protection. Certain omissions of, or defects in, the notice of copyright, however, could have led to loss of copyright protection if steps were not taken to correct or cure the omissions or defects. The Copyright Office has issued a final regulation (37 CFR 201.20) that suggests various acceptable positions for the notice of copyright.

For further information, write to the Copyright Office and request Circular 3, *Copyright Notice,* and Circular 96, Section 201.20, *Methods of Affixation and Positions of the Copyright Notice on Various Types of Works.*

Works Already in the Public Domain

Neither the 1976 Copyright Act, the Berne Convention Implementation Act of 1988, the Copyright Renewal Act of 1992, nor the Sonny Bono Copyright Term Extension Act of 1998 will restore protection to works that fell into the public domain before the passage of the laws. However, the North American Free Trade Agreement Implementation Act (NAFTA) and the Uruguay Round Agreements Act (URAA) may restore copyright in certain works of foreign origin that were in the public domain in the United States. Under the copyright law in effect prior to January 1, 1978, copyright could be lost in several situations. The most common were publication without the required notice of copyright, expiration of the first 28-year term without renewal, or final expiration of the second copyright term. The Copyright Renewal Act of 1992 automatically renews first term copyrights secured between January 1, 1964, and December 31, 1977.

Scope of Exclusive Rights Under Copyright

The present law has changed and enlarged in some cases the scope of the copyright owner's rights. The new rights apply to all uses of a work subject to protection by copyright after January 1, 1978, regardless of when the work was created.

Duration of Copyright Protection

Works Originally Copyrighted On or After January 1, 1978

A work that is created and fixed in tangible form for the first time on or after January 1, 1978, is automatically protected from the moment of its creation and is ordinarily given a term enduring for the author's life plus an additional 70 years after the author's death. In the case of "a joint work prepared by two or more authors who did not work for hire," the term lasts for 70 years after the last surviving author's death. For works made for hire and for anonymous and pseudonymous works (unless the author's identity is revealed in the Copyright Office records), the duration of copyright will be 95 years from publication or 120 years from creation, whichever is less.

Works created before the 1976 law came into effect but neither published nor registered for copyright before January 1, 1978, have been automatically brought under the statute and are now given federal copyright protection. The duration of copyright in these works will generally be computed in the same way as for new works: the life-plus-70 or 95/120-year terms will apply. However, all works in this category are guaranteed at least 25 years of statutory protection.

Works Copyrighted Before January 1, 1978

Under the law in effect before 1978, copyright was secured either on the date a work was published with notice of copyright or on the date of registration if the work was registered in unpublished form. In either case, copyright endured for a first term of 28 years from the date on which it was secured. During the last (28th) year of the first term, the copyright was eligible for renewal. The copyright law extends the renewal term from 28 to 67 years for copyrights in existence on January 1, 1978.

However, for works copyrighted prior to January 1, 1964, the copyright still must have been renewed in the 28th calendar year to receive the 67-year period of added protection. The amending legislation enacted June 26, 1992, automatically extends this second term for works first copyrighted between January 1, 1964, and December 31, 1977. For more detailed information on the copyright term, write or call the Copyright Office and request Circular 15A, *Duration of Copyright*, and Circular 15T, *Extension of Copyright Terms*.

Works First Published Before 1978: the Copyright Notice

General Information About the Copyright Notice

In investigating the copyright status of works first published before January 1, 1978, the most important thing to look for is the notice of copyright. As a general rule under the previous law, copyright protection was lost permanently if the notice was omitted from the first authorized published edition of a work or if it appeared in the wrong form or position. The form and position of the copyright notice for various types of works were specified in the copyright statute. Some courts were liberal in overlooking relatively minor departures from the statutory requirements, but a basic failure to comply with the notice provisions forfeited copyright protection and put the work into the public domain in this country.

Absence of Copyright Notice

For works first published before 1978, the complete absence of a copyright notice from a published copy generally indicates that the work is not protected by copyright. For works first published before March 1, 1989, the copyright notice is mandatory, but omission could have been cured by registration before or within 5 years of publication and by adding the notice to copies published in the United States after dis-

covery of the omission. Some works may contain a notice, others may not. The absence of a notice in works published on or after March 1, 1989, does not necessarily indicate that the work is in the public domain.

Unpublished Works · No notice of copyright was required on the copies of any unpublished work. The concept of "publication" is very technical, and it was possible for a number of copies lacking a copyright notice to be reproduced and distributed without affecting copyright protection.

Foreign Editions · In the case of works seeking *ad interim* copyright,* copies of a copyrighted work were exempted from the notice requirements if they were first published outside the United States. Some copies of these foreign editions could find their way into the United States without impairing the copyright.

* NOTE: *"Ad interim* copyright" refers to a special short term of copyright available to certain pre-1978 books and periodicals. For further information on *ad interim* copyright, see page 8.

Accidental Omission · The 1909 statute preserved copyright protection if the notice was omitted by accident or mistake from a "particular copy or copies."

Unauthorized Publication · A valid copyright was not secured if someone deleted the notice and/or published the work without authorization from the copyright owner.

Sound Recordings · Reproductions of sound recordings usually contain two different types of creative works: the underlying musical, dramatic, or literary work that is being performed or read and the fixation of the actual sounds embodying the performance or reading. For protection of the underlying musical or literary work embodied in a recording, it is not necessary that a copyright notice covering this material appear on the phonograph records or tapes on which the recording is reproduced. As noted above, a special notice is required for protection of the recording of a series of musical, spoken, or other sounds that were fixed on or after February 15, 1972. Sound recordings fixed before February 15, 1972, are not eligible for federal copyright protection. The Sound Recording Act of 1971, the present copyright law, and the Berne Convention Implementation Act of 1988 cannot be applied or be construed to provide any retroactive protection for sound recordings fixed before February 15, 1972. Such works, however, may be protected by various state laws or doctrines of common law.

The Date in the Copyright Notice

If you find a copyright notice, the date it contains may be important in determining the copyright status of the work. In general, the notice on works published before 1978 must include the year in which copyright was secured by publication or, if the work was first registered for copyright in unpublished form, the year in which registration was made. There are two main exceptions to this rule.

1. For pictorial, graphic, or sculptural works (Classes F through K under the 1909 law), the law permitted omission of the year date in the notice.

2. For "new versions" of previously published or copyrighted works, the notice was not usually required to include more than the year of first publication of the new version itself. This is explained further under "Derivative Works" below.

The year in the notice usually (though not always) indicated when the copyright began. It is, therefore, significant in determining whether a copyright is still in effect; or, if the copyright has not yet run its course, the year date will help in deciding when the copyright is scheduled to expire. For further information about the duration of copyright, request Circular 15A, *Duration of Copyright*.

In evaluating the meaning of the date in a notice, you should keep the following points in mind:

Works Published and Copyrighted Before January 1, 1978 · A work published before January 1, 1978, and copyrighted within the past 75 years may still be protected by copyright in the United States if a valid renewal registration was made during the 28th year of the first term of the copyright. If renewed by registration or under the Copyright Renewal Act of 1992 and if still valid under the other provisions of the law, the copyright will expire 95 years from the end of the year in which it was first secured.

Therefore, the U.S. copyright in any work published or copyrighted prior to January 1, 1923, has expired by operation of law, and the work has permanently fallen into the public domain in the United States. For example, on January 1, 1997, copyrights in works first published or copyrighted before January 1, 1922, have expired; on January 1, 1998, copyrights in works first published or copyrighted before January 1, 1923, have expired. Unless the copyright law is changed again, no works under protection on January 1, 1999, will fall into the public domain in the United States until January 1, 2019.

Works First Published or Copyrighted Between January 1, 1923, and December 31, 1949, But Not Renewed · If a work was first published or copyrighted between January 1, 1923, and December 31, 1949, it is important to determine whether the copyright was renewed during the last (28th) year of the first term of the copyright. This can be done by searching the Copyright Office records or catalogs as explained previously. If no renewal registration was made, copyright protection expired permanently at the end of the 28th year of the year date it was first secured.

Works First Published or Copyrighted Between January 1, 1923, and December 31, 1949, and Registered for Renewal · When a valid renewal registration was made and copyright in the work was in its second term on December 31, 1977, the renewal copyright term was extended under the latest act to 67 years. In these cases, copyright will last for a total of 95 years from the end of the year in which copyright was originally secured. Example: Copyright in a work first published in 1925 and renewed in 1953 will expire on December 31, 2020.

Works First Published or Copyrighted Between January 1, 1950, and December 31, 1963 · If a work was in its first 28-year term of copyright protection on January 1, 1978, it must have been renewed in a timely fashion to have secured the maximum term of copyright protection. If renewal registration was made during the 28th calendar year of its first term, copyright would endure for 95 years from the end of the year copyright was originally secured. If not renewed, the copyright expired at the end of its 28th calendar year.

Works First Published or Copyrighted Between January 1, 1964, and December 31, 1977 · If a work was in its first 28-year term of copyright protection on June 26, 1992, renewal registration is now optional. The term of copyright for works published or copyrighted during this time period has been extended to 95 years by the Copyright Renewal Act of 1992 and the Sonny Bono Term Extension Act of 1998. There is no need to make the renewal filing to extend the original 28-year copyright term to the full 95 years.

However, there are several advantages to making a renewal registration during the 28th year of the original term of copyright. If renewal registration is made during the 28th year of the original term of copyright, the renewal copyright vests in the name of the renewal claimant on the effective date of the renewal registration; the renewal certificate constitutes *prima facie* evidence as to the validity of the copyright during the renewed and extended term and of the facts stated in the certificate; and, the right to use the derivative work in the extended term may be affected. Request Circular 15, *Renewal of Copyright*, for further information.

Unpublished, Unregistered Works · Before 1978, if a work had been neither "published" in the legal sense nor registered in the Copyright Office, it was subject to perpetual protection under the common law. On January 1, 1978, all works of this kind, subject to protection by copyright, were automatically brought under the federal copyright statute. The duration of copyright for these works can vary, but none of them will expire before December 31, 2002.

Derivative Works

In examining a copy (or a record, disk, or tape) for copyright information, it is important to determine whether that particular version of the work is an original edition of the work or a "new version." New versions include musical arrangements, adaptations, revised or newly edited editions, translations, dramatizations, abridgments, compilations, and works republished with new matter added. The law provides that derivative works, published or unpublished, are independently copyrightable and that the copyright in such a work does not affect or extend the protection, if any, in the underlying work. Under the 1909 law, courts have also held that the notice of copyright on a derivative work ordinarily need not include the dates or other information pertaining to the earlier works incorporated in it. This principle is specifically preserved in the present copyright law. Thus, if the copy (or the record, disk, or tape) constitutes a derivative version of the work, these points should be kept in mind:

- The date in the copyright notice is not necessarily an indication of when copyright in all the material in the work will expire. Some of the material may already be in the public domain, and some parts of the work may expire sooner than others.

- Even if some of the material in the derivative work is in the public domain and free for use, this does not mean that the "new" material added to it can be used without permission from the owner of copyright in the derivative work. It may be necessary to compare editions to determine what is free to use and what is not.

- Ownership of rights in the material included in a derivative work and in the preexisting work upon which it may be based may differ, and permission obtained from the owners of certain parts of the work may not authorize the use of other parts.

The Name in the Copyright Notice

Under the copyright statute in effect before 1978, the notice was required to include "the name of the copyright proprietor." The present act requires that the notice include "the name of the owner of copyright in the work, or an abbreviation by which the name can be recognized, or a generally known alternative designation of the owner." The name in the notice (sometimes in combination with the other statements on the copy, records, disk, tape, container, or label) often gives persons wishing to use the work the information needed to identify the owner from whom licenses or permission can be sought. In other cases, the name provides a starting point for a search in the Copyright Office records or catalogs, as explained at the beginning of this circular.

In the case of works published before 1978, copyright registration is made in the name of the individual person or the entity identified as the copyright owner in the notice. For works published on or after January 1, 1978, registration is made in the name of the person or entity owning all the rights on the date the registration is made. This may or may not be the name appearing in the notice. In addition to its records of copyright registration, the Copyright Office maintains extensive records of assignments, exclusive licenses, and other documents dealing with copyright ownership.

Ad Interim

Ad interim copyright was a special short-term copyright that applied to certain books and periodicals in the English language that were first manufactured and published outside the United States. It was a partial exception to the manufacturing requirements of the previous U.S. copyright law. Its purpose was to secure temporary U.S. protection for a work, pending the manufacture of an edition in the United States. The *ad interim* requirements changed several times over the years and were subject to a number of exceptions and qualifications.

The manufacturing provisions of the copyright act expired on July 1, 1986, and are no longer a part of the copyright law. The transitional and supplementary provisions of the act provide that for any work in which *ad interim* copyright was subsisting or capable of being secured on December 31, 1977, copyright protection would be extended for a term compatible with the other works in which copyright was subsisting on the effective date of the new act. Consequently, if the work was first published on or after July 1, 1977, and was eligible for *ad interim* copyright protection, the provisions of the present copyright act will be applicable to the protection of these works. Anyone investigating the copyright status of an English-language book or periodical first published outside the United States before July 1, 1977, should check carefully to determine:

- Whether the manufacturing requirements were applicable to the work; and
- If so, whether the *ad interim* requirements were met.

For Further Information

Information via the Internet

Frequently requested circulars, announcements, regulations, other related materials, and all copyright application forms are available via the Internet. You may access these from the Copyright Office website at *www.copyright.gov.*

Information by fax

Circulars and other information (but not application forms) are available by using a touchtone phone to access Fax-on-Demand at (202) 707-2600.

Information by telephone

For general information about copyright, call the Copyright Public Information Office at (202) 707-3000. The TTY number is (202) 707-6737. Information specialists are on duty from 8:30 a.m. to 5:00 p.m., eastern time, Monday through Friday, except federal holidays. Recorded information is available 24 hours a day. Or, if you know which application forms and circulars you want, request them 24 hours a day from the Forms and Publications Hotline at (202) 707-9100. Leave a recorded message.

Information by regular mail

Write to:

*Library of Congress
Copyright Office
Publications Section, LM -455
101 Independence Avenue, S.E.
Washington, D.C. 20559-6000*

 # Search Request Form

Library of Congress
Copyright Office
101 Independence Avenue SE
Washington, D.C. 20559-6000

Reference & Bibliography Section
8:30 a.m. to 5 p.m. eastern
Monday through Friday,
Phone: (202) 707-6850
Fax: (202) 252-3485

TYPE OF WORK

☐ Book ☐ Music ☐ Motion Picture ☐ Drama ☐ Sound Recording ☐ Computer Program
☐ Photograph/Artwork ☐ Map ☐ Periodical ☐ Contribution ☐ Architectural Work ☐ Mask Work

SEARCH INFORMATION YOU REQUIRE

☐ Registration ☐ Renewal ☐ Assignment ☐ Address

SPECIFICS OF WORK TO BE SEARCHED

Title _____

_____

Author _____

_____

Copyright claimant _____
(Name in © notice)

Approximate year date of publication/creation _____

Registration Number (if known) _____

If you need more space please attach additional pages.

Estimates are based on the Copyright Office fee of $75* an *hour or fraction of an hour* consumed. The more information you furnish as a basis for the search, the better service we can provide. The time between the date of receipt of your fee for the search and your receiving a report will vary from 8 to 12 weeks depending on workload.

Names, titles, and short phrases are not copyrightable.

Please read Circular 22 for more information on copyright searches.

Your name _____ Date _____

Address _____

_____

Daytime telephone _____ Convey results of estimate/search by telephone ☐ Yes ☐ No

Fee enclosed? ☐ Yes: AMOUNT: $ _____ ☐ No

NOTE: Copyright Office fees are subject to change. For current fees, check the Copyright Office website at *www.copyright.gov*, write the Copyright Office, or call (202) 707-3000.

U.S. Copyright Office · The Library of Congress · 101 Independence Avenue SE · Washington, DC 20559-6000 · www.copyright.gov

CIRCULAR 22   PRINT REV: 01/2004—30,000   WEB REV: 01/2004   Printed on recycled paper   U.S. GOVERNMENT PRINTING OFFICE: 2004-304-447/60,084

 # Search Request Form

Library of Congress
Copyright Office
101 Independence Avenue SE
Washington, D.C. 20559-6000

Reference & Bibliography Section
8:30 a.m. to 5 p.m. eastern
Monday through Friday,
Phone: (202) 707-6850
Fax: (202) 252-3485

TYPE OF WORK

☐ Book ☐ Music ☐ Motion Picture ☐ Drama ☐ Sound Recording ☐ Computer Program
☐ Photograph/Artwork ☐ Map ☐ Periodical ☐ Contribution ☐ Architectural Work ☐ Mask Work

SEARCH INFORMATION YOU REQUIRE

☐ Registration ☐ Renewal ☐ Assignment ☐ Address

SPECIFICS OF WORK TO BE SEARCHED

Title _____

_____

Author _____

_____

Copyright claimant _____
(Name in © notice)

Approximate year date of publication/creation _____

Registration Number (if known) _____

If you need more space please attach additional pages.

Estimates are based on the Copyright Office fee of $75* an *hour or fraction of an hour* consumed. The more information you furnish as a basis for the search, the better service we can provide. The time between the date of receipt of your fee for the search and your receiving a report will vary from 8 to 12 weeks depending on workload.

Names, titles, and short phrases are not copyrightable.

Please read Circular 22 for more information on copyright searches.

Your name _____ Date _____

Address _____

_____

Daytime telephone _____ Convey results of estimate/search by telephone ☐ Yes ☐ No

Fee enclosed? ☐ Yes: AMOUNT: $ _____ ☐ No

NOTE: Copyright Office fees are subject to change. For current fees, check the Copyright Office website at *www.copyright.gov*, write the Copyright Office, or call (202) 707-3000.

Printed in the United States
71157LV00002B/34

9 781600 371387